Oliver Goldsmith

Merrill's English Texts

THE DESERTED VILLAGE
THE TRAVELER
AND OTHER POEMS

BY

OLIVER GOLDSMITH

EDITED WITH AN INTRODUCTION AND NOTES
BY EDNA H. L. TURPIN, AUTHOR OF "STORIES
FROM AMERICAN HISTORY," "CLASSIC
FABLES," "FAMOUS PAINTERS," ETC., ETC.

WILDSIDE PRESS

CONTENTS

PUBLISHERS' NOTE

Merrill's English Texts

THIS series of books will include in complete editions those masterpieces of English Literature that are best adapted for the use of schools and colleges. The editors of the several volumes will be chosen for their special qualifications in connection with the texts to be issued under their individual supervision, but familiarity with the practical needs of the classroom, no less than sound scholarship, will characterize the editing of every book in the series.

In connection with each text, a critical and historical introduction, including a sketch of the life of the author and his relation to the thought of his time, critical opinions of the work in question chosen from the great body of English criticism, and, where possible, a portrait of the author, will be given. Ample explanatory notes of such passages in the text as call for special attention will be supplied, but irrelevant annotation and explanations of the obvious will be rigidly excluded.

CHARLES E. MERRILL CO.

INTRODUCTION

OLIVER GOLDSMITH

NOT the least charm of Goldsmith's books is the intimate relation into which they bring us with one of the most "kind, artless, good humored, excursive, sensible, whimsical, intelligent beings" in the world of letters. His character is reflected in his writings, as in a mirror; and the events of his life are repeated in the incidents of his tales and poems and in the plots of his comedies. Others might have made a tragedy of life with such privations, such struggles, such pathos, such bitterness even; but our gentle humorist turned it into comedy.

Oliver Goldsmith came of a family "all equally generous, credulous, simple." His father, Reverend Charles Goldsmith, was an Irish curate, the original of the preacher of *The Deserted Village*, and Dr. Primrose of *The Vicar of Wakefield*. The pious, unworldly scholar gave his five sons and three daughters characteristic training. His son, as "the Man in Black," tells us he "took as much care to form our morals as to improve our understanding; . . . he wound us up to be mere machines of pity, and rendered us incapable of withstanding the slightest impulse made either by real or fictitious distress. In a word, we were perfectly instructed in the art of giving away thousands before we were taught the necessary qualification of getting a farthing."

Oliver, the second son, was born the tenth of November, 1728, in the Irish village of Pallas, where Charles Goldsmith was then a curate, "passing rich with forty pounds a year." The family fortunes improved, and when Oliver was two years old his father moved to the village of Lissoy. At Lissoy, said to be the original of Auburn in *The Deserted Village*, Oliver's childhood was spent. At the age of three he was sent to a dame-school to be taught his letters and kept out of harm's way. Neither task was easy. From the first he showed a taste for mischief and a distaste for study, which brought from his mistress the verdict that "a dull boy he was." At six he was put under the tuition — "under the ferule" according to the suggestive phrase of the day — of the village schoolmaster. Here, also, he showed himself "a stupid heavy blockhead, little better than a fool." Oliver learned more from his schoolmaster's character and experience than from his books. Thomas, or Paddy, Byrne was an old soldier, a traveler, a poet or rhymester, learned in the lore of ghosts and fairies, voluble about war and adventure. His tales found an eager listener in Oliver, and this schoolmaster was one of the guiding influences of the boy's young imagination. Like his master, he began to write verse, and these stray rhymes were received by his mother as proof that he was not the stupid fellow he was so often called. His father intended him for a trade, but maternal urgency prevailed, and it was resolved to send him to college.

Oliver's preparatory schooling was interrupted by a violent attack of smallpox, which left its marks for life upon his face and upon his character. That ugly, scarred face, that thickset, awkward figure, was a trying mask for the gentle, sensitive nature — a mask against which it often and vainly rebelled. Oliver's earliest witticisms of which we have account were retorts to comments on his personal appearance. An uncle, said to lack integrity as well as tact, eyed him closely on their first meeting after his illness.

"Why, Noll," he exclaimed, "you are become a fright! When do you mean to get handsome again?"

The boy blushed and shuffled in silent confusion, and the question was repeated. Then he answered with a meaning flash of the eye, "I mean to get better, sir, when you do."

From Paddy Byrne's tuition, Oliver passed to other schools, — Elphinstone, Athlone, and Edgeworthstown. An incident of a journey between Edgeworthstown and his home at Lissoy, twenty miles away, deserves to be chronicled. Goldsmith, then a lad of fifteen, was making the journey on horseback, jubilant in possession of unaccustomed wealth, — a guinea presented by a friend. The money burned in his pocket, — for with him to have was ever to spend. He resolved, instead of making the journey in a day, to stay overnight at an inn. Meeting a man on the road, he asked "what was the best house of the neighborhood," meaning house of public entertainment. The man, a wag, who was amused by the youth's self-consequence, gravely directed him to what was indeed the "best house" — the private mansion of the squire. Oliver here played the man, ordered a good supper and a hot cake for breakfast, and insisted on treating his supposed landlord and his family. The squire was himself a man of humor, and, moreover, he learned that the lad was the son of his old acquaintance, Reverend Charles Goldsmith. He carried on the joke, and it was not until he wished to settle his bill next morning that Oliver learned to his embarrassment that he had been entertained at a private house. This incident, like many other events of his life, was turned to literary account; it was the groundwork of his successful comedy, *She Stoops to Conquer; or, The Mistakes of a Night.*

Reverend Charles Goldsmith's income was so taxed with heavy family expenses that he was unable to support his son at college. Oliver entered Trinity College, Dublin, in 1745, as a "sizar," or charity scholar. Instead of paying money for board and lodging — if so we may term left-over food and a garret room — he performed certain menial offices, such as sweeping the college courts, and carrying food from the kitchen to the dining hall. A sizar's dress — a coarse black gown and a flat cap — was a badge of his office, his inferior position, — a galling one, we well may imagine, to the shy youth with his "exquisite sensibility of contempt." Goldsmith was unhappy, too, in being consigned to the care of a tutor of uncongenial temper and tastes. Wilder was an impatient, overbearing man of violent temper, interested in mathematics and logic. Goldsmith was indolent if not stupid, averse to mathematics, fond of languages and letters.

His father was so little able to aid him financially, that he was almost entirely dependent on his good uncle Contarine, a country curate of unlimited generosity but limited means. When Oliver's purse was empty, — a frequent case with the poor and improvident youth, — he would sometimes earn a few shillings by writing a song or ballad for a Dublin printer. Not the least of his reward was the delight as he loitered about the streets at night, of hearing his verses from the lips of street singers. Often, before he returned to his college garret, he had spent or given away the last penny of his little earnings. On one evening's stroll a poor woman appealed to him for food and shelter for her five little ones. Goldsmith had no money, but what he had he gave, — the coat from his back, the blankets from his bed, and he in turn had to be succored by his college mates next day.

The great statesman, Edmund Burke, was one of Oliver

Goldsmith's college mates at Dublin. But they moved in different circles in their little world, and did not become acquaintances and friends until they met in the literary world of London.

Reverend Charles Goldsmith died in 1747, leaving his widow a bare support, and Oliver's only resource was the bounty of his uncle Contarine. He finished his college course, however, and, at the foot of his class, left Dublin in February, 1749, a Bachelor of Arts.

He left college. but he had no longer a home to which to turn. The Lissoy cottage, dear to his childhood and youth, had passed from the family at his father's death. His mother, straitened in means, had retired with her daughters to a little cottage at Ballymahon. His uncle Contarine and his brother Henry were both curates with small incomes and families of their own. But their hearts and houses were open to the idle, lovable fellow whose college career must have been a great disappointment to them all. They urged upon him now the necessity of choosing a profession and of preparing himself for it.

Rather in accordance with the wishes of his family than with his own inclination, it was decided that Oliver should follow the example of his father and brother and become a clergyman. As he whimsically said, he had no fancy for the somber color of a clergyman's clothes, — and, as he said about reading prayers in later years, he "did not think himself good enough." Still he accepted this choice of a profession. On account of his youth, it was necessary to defer for two years his entrance into the sacred office. Instead of spending this time in preparatory studies, Goldsmith amused himself visiting relatives and friends, fishing, hunting, frolicking at inns, reading nothing graver than volumes of travels, poems, novels, and plays. It is small wonder that when he presented himself before the bishop he was rejected. The immediate cause of rejection is a matter of no moment — whether, as some assert, he appeared in "flaming scarlet breeches," whether there were unsatisfactory reports from his old tutor, or whether he was found wanting in the required preparatory studies. He was unfit for the office; the bishop recognized his unfitness.

On his friends again devolved the task of finding him a vocation, and his uncle Contarine secured him a place as tutor in a gentleman's family. Its duties proved uncongenial. Goldsmith soon quarreled with his employer and left him, but carried away, as his salary, the unheard-of wealth of thirty pounds. For six weeks he disappeared from the view of his friends; then he reappeared — without the thirty pounds. That had gone at cards and merry-making. His relatives were naturally angry and indignant at his conduct, but a peace was patched up, and again the family conclave assembled to choose him a profession. This time law was decided upon, and patient uncle Contarine furnished funds for him to go to London to pursue legal studies. Oliver bade his friends farewell and went — as far as Dublin, where his pockets were emptied by sharpers. Again he returned home, again he was forgiven, again a profession was chosen for him. In the autumn of 1752 he left Ireland to study medicine in Edinburgh. His light heart would have grown heavy could he have known that he had looked his last upon his mother, his brother Henry, his good uncle Contarine, upon "sweet Lissoy" and the scenes dear to his childhood. Often and lovingly in days to come his heart was to turn toward Ireland, but never his vagrant footsteps.

Oliver's first experience in Edinburgh was thoroughly characteristic. He engaged lodgings, then sallied forth to see the sights of the city. Not until he wished to return to his room did he realize that he had neglected to learn the name of his landlady or the street and number of her house. By a fortunate chance he came upon the porter who had carried his luggage and was rescued from this predicament.

We know nothing of Goldsmith's life in Edinburgh except from one or two pleasant letters to friends and from some tailor's bill for "silver Hatt-Lace," "Sky-Blew Sattin," and "Claret-coloured Cloth," finery dear to his heart. We have no reason to suppose that in Edinburgh he devoted himself more assiduously to study than in Dublin. He gave at least nominal attention to his class work, and in the course of time announced his wish to go abroad to pursue the study of medicine in France and Holland. His uncle Contarine granted the desired permission and the needed pecuniary aid. In the spring of 1754, Goldsmith went to Leyden, where he remained about a year, attending some lectures on chemistry and anatomy. His small store of money was soon exhausted, and he resorted to various shifts to earn a living, — among others, to teaching the English language to Dutchmen, — not directly, for he knew no Dutch, but by means of his smattering of French.

After a few months in Leyden, a generous Irish friend furnished him money to go to Paris to pursue his medical studies. On the eve of leaving Leyden he strolled into a florist's garden; the gorgeous array of tulips reminded him of his uncle Contarine's fondness for that flower, then fashionable and costly in the extreme. His purse was out in an instant, and the money borrowed for his journey was spent in rare bulbs for his uncle. He left Leyden on foot, "with only one clean shirt and no money in his pocket." In the adventures of George Primrose in *The Vicar of Wakefield*, Goldsmith gives, in the main, an ac-

count of his wanderings in Europe.   On foot he traveled
through Germany, France, Switzerland, Italy, — now
sleeping in a barn, now sheltered in a peasant's cottage,
paying for a dinner with a song, a supper with a tune on
his flute, a lodging with an harangue on philosophy. For
a while he was tutor to a miserly young Englishman, who
could have taught him financial wisdom had it been in his
power to learn.

In Italy tidings came to him of the severe illness of his
good uncle Contarine. We have a personal sense of regret
that the kind uncle's sacrifices and loyal faith were not
rewarded by the sight of the success and fame of his
nephew, that he died while Oliver was little better than an
unknown vagabond. There is some comfort in the fact
that he did not lack testimonials of his nephew's affection,
such as the tulip bulbs for which Oliver went footsore.

Perhaps this tidings determined Goldsmith's return to
England. He set his face homeward, "walking from city
to city, examining mankind more nearly and seeing both
sides of the picture." In February, 1756, he landed in
Dover, with an empty purse and with a degree in medicine,
where and how acquired we do not know. What treasures
of thought and experience he had gained, of which later,
in inimitable essay, poem, play, and story, he was to make
us the heir!

Probably in 1756 Goldsmith looked on himself as did·
his friends, in a far different light from that in which he
appears to us to-day. His father, mother, brother, uncle,
and friends had struggled to educate and maintain him.
His school and college life had been discreditable; he
had attempted each one of the learned professions in turn,
and in turn had failed in each. He was now coming back
from a gypsy-like tramp, a journey such as a peddler
might have taken. At twenty-eight, then, he was a failure,

having "nothing but his brogue and his blunders," — for one did not count his ability to write a charming letter, or his possession of that wonderful treasure, a literary style.

How Goldsmith earned his livelihood during his first months in England, we do not know. We have some reason to think that he took trifling parts in comedies and acted as usher in a school.

"You may easily imagine," he wrote later in a letter, "what difficulties I had to encounter, left as I was without friends, recommendations, money, or impudence."

He drifted to London, and there, after serving for a while as an apothecary's assistant, he began to practice medicine. His patients were few and humble, his rewards small, but he tried to put the best foot foremost with his friends, and informed them that "he was practicing physic and doing very well." One of his biographers gives a humorous incident of these days. Goldsmith had somehow managed to procure the black coat which, with a wig and a cane, was the professional attire of a physician. "The coat was a second-hand one of rusty velvet, with a patch on the left breast which he adroitly covered with his three-cornered hat during his medical visits; and we have an amusing anecdote of his contest of courtesy with a patient who persisted in endeavoring to relieve him from the hat, which only made him press it more devoutly to his heart."

His success and rewards in the medical world were so small that he accepted the offer of a friend to take temporary charge of a school. Here he met Mr. Griffiths, a bookseller, who had established a periodical called *The Monthly Review*. Goldsmith's remarks on literary subjects showed taste and ability, and led Griffiths to offer him an humble position on the *Review*. He gave up his school work, and eked out existence by translations, reviews, criticisms, and miscellaneous contributions to periodicals. After a few months of this life, he was glad to leave his attic and return to the school of his friend, Dr. Milner. Through Dr. Milner's influence he hoped to secure a medical appointment in India. To defray the necessary expenses, Goldsmith — working now, as always, under the spur of necessity — wrote a clever but rather presumptuous treatise, *Enquiry into the Present State of Polite Learning in Europe.*

Goldsmith was actually appointed physician and surgeon to a factory in Coromandel and — there the matter ended. The position was transferred to another person, whether on account of Goldsmith's inefficiency or on account of his lack of influence we can only conjecture. That it was not because he had given up the plan of a medical career, is certain. A short time after this he presented himself at Surgeon's Hall to be examined for the office of hospital mate. The college book for December 21, 1758, bears a record which may throw light on the Coromandel affair: "James Bernard, mate to an hospital. Oliver Goldsmith found not qualified for ditto."

Thus necessity more than inclination turned Goldsmith to literature as a profession. He had to rely for a support on hack work — reviews, criticisms, and memoirs.

His *Enquiry*, published in 1759, had attracted some attention, from authors and booksellers especially, and led to his being asked to contribute to several periodicals. For one of these he wrote his *Chinese Letters*, afterwards remodeled and published under the title of *The Citizen of the World.* In a series of charming papers, somewhat on the order of those contributed by Addison to *The Spectator*, Goldsmith purported to give the experiences and reflections of a Chinese scholar on a visit to London. "Few works exhibit a nicer perception, a more delicate delineation of life and manners. Wit, humor, and sentiment pervade every page; the vices and follies of the day are touched with the most perfect and diverting satire; and English characteristics in endless variety are hit off with the pencil of a master." Had the hack of Green Arbor Court written nothing else, these *Letters* would have given him a worthy and enduring place in English literature.

The success of the *Letters* enabled Goldsmith to leave his attic in Green Arbor Court — furnished with "a mean bed and a single wooden chair" — for better quarters in Wine Office Court. Here, in May, 1761, began his acquaintance with Dr. Johnson. Johnson had come to London years before, as poor as Goldsmith, and hampered, moreover, by physical infirmity and mental gloom. Overbearing all obstacles, he had carried out his resolution "to fight my way by my literature and my wit." His *Dictionary,* his *Rambler,* his *Rasselas,* had put him in the forefront of men of letters, and his conversational and critical powers made him the literary dictator of the day. It was arranged that Dr. Percy should call to bring him to a literary supper given by Goldsmith in his new apartments. Dr. Percy "was much struck by the studied neatness of Johnson's dress: he had on a new suit of clothes, a new wig nicely powdered, and everything about him was so dissimilar from his usual habits and appearance that his companion could not help enquiring the cause of this singular transformation. 'Why, sir,' said Johnson, 'I hear that Goldsmith, who is a very great sloven, justifies his disregard of cleanliness and decency by quoting my practice, and I am desirous this night to show him a better example.'"

The acquaintance begun that night ripened into intimacy and warm friendship. Johnson gave Goldsmith much good advice — which was generally disregarded — and substantial aid. Up those stairs in Wine Office

Court came many famous men besides Johnson, — Smollett, Richardson, Gray, Young, Percy, Akenside, Shenstone, Walpole, Chesterfield, Burke, Garrick, Reynolds. The circle of Goldsmith's friends included most of the scholars and notable men of the day. He loved society, although he cut but a poor figure in it. His ugly face, his ungainly figure decked out in gay silks and velvets, his awkward, hesitating manner, made him often an object of ridicule. Even his friends, who appreciated his good humor and generosity and admired his genius, could not sometimes resist the temptation of making his credulity and simple vanity the butt of their witticisms. Perhaps his happiest hours, after all, were spent in that gentle genial company which he drew around himself — the Man in Black, Tony Lumpkin, the Primroses — whom he has left to cheer and delight thousands of other hearts.

For some years after the success of the *Letters*, Goldsmith was kept busy with what he called "book building," that is, abridgments and compendiums. One of these was *A Compendium of Biography for Young People*, based upon Plutarch's *Lives;* another was *The History of England in a Series of Letters from a Nobleman to his Son*, which became exceedingly popular.

Through the friendship of Johnson and Reynolds, Goldsmith was one of the nine original members of the famous Literary Club, founded by them in 1764. There was, we are told, some demur in the Club when it was first proposed to admit him. "As he wrote for the booksellers," said Sir John Hawkins, "we of the Club looked upon him as a mere literary drudge, equal to the task of compiling and translating, but little capable of original and still less of poetical composition."

Dr. Johnson was a better judge of Goldsmith's ability,

though displayed in a limited field. "Dr. Goldsmith, sir," he said as early as 1763 to his sycophant Boswell, "is one of the first men we now have as an author."

For some years Goldsmith had on hand a didactic poem on which he wrote or blotted couplets, a few at a time, as fancy moved him. "Either Reynolds or a mutual friend who immediately communicated the story to him, calling at the lodgings of the poet, opened the door without ceremony and discovered him, not in meditation or in the throes of poetic birth, but in the boyish office of teaching a favorite dog to sit upright upon its haunches, or, as it is commonly said, to beg. Occasionally he glanced his eye over his desk and occasionally shook his finger at his unwilling pupil in order to make him retain his position, while on the page before him was written that couplet, with the ink of the second line still wet, from the description of Italy:—

> " ' By sports like these are all their cares beguil'd,
> The sports of children satisfy the child.'

Something of consonance between the verses and the writer's occupation seems at once to have struck the visitor, and Goldsmith frankly admitted that the one had suggested the other." This poem was published in December, 1764, under the title of *The Traveller; or, A Prospect of Society. A Poem*. It is an excellent example of the eighteenth-century didactic poem. The author represents himself as sitting upon an Alpine height and moralizing about the social and political condition of the countries spread out before him. People so little expected such a masterpiece as this charming poem from "the bookseller's drudge," that some of them attributed it to his friend, Dr. Johnson; the question as to its authorship was settled by Johnson himself, who, moreover, pro-

nounced the poem "the finest poem that had appeared
since the days of Pope." He read it aloud to Miss Rey-
nolds, who had toasted Goldsmith as the ugliest man of
her acquaintance. "Well," she exclaimed, "I never more
shall think Dr. Goldsmith ugly."

The Traveller went through edition after edition and
brought large rewards to the publishers, but to the author
himself only twenty-one pounds.

Sir John Hawkins gives with undisguised irritation an
incident showing Goldsmith's lack of worldly wisdom.
The poet was asked to visit the Duke of Northumberland
and "his lordship told of his pleasure in reading *The
Traveller* and said that he was going Lord-Lieutenant of
Ireland, and hearing that I was a native of that country,
he should be glad to do me any kindness."

Sir John eagerly inquired what Goldsmith answered.

"Why, I could say nothing," answered the poet, "but
that I had a brother there, a clergyman, that stood in
need of help : as for myself, I have no dependence on the
promises of great men : I look to the booksellers for sup-
port; they are my best friends, and I am not inclined to
forsake them for others."

"Thus," exclaims his worldly-wise friend, "did this
idiot in the affairs of the world trifle with his fortune
and put back the hand that was held out to assist him."
We breathe a sigh of relief that Goldsmith was Gold-
smith — free-hearted, independent, magnanimous — and
pass on.

If the poet did not know how to ask favors, he was sur-
rounded by those who did. He had a constant levee of his
distressed countrymen, whose wants, so far as he was able,
he always relieved; and he has often been known to have
left himself without a guinea in order to supply the neces-
sities of others.

Impatient of the small pecuniary rewards of his literary labors, Goldsmith again turned his thoughts to a medical career. But in vain he sported his wig and gold-headed cane. Patients were not to be had, and he finally put aside the rôle of physician and henceforth accepted that of man of letters. He worked by fits and starts on hack work, abridgments of history and biography, the money for which was too often spent before it was received.

Two years after the publication of *The Traveller* there appeared another original work which won Goldsmith fame in a new field. This was *The Vicar of Wakefield.* Boswell gives us "from Johnson's own exact narration" a famous account of the sale of the manuscript. Johnson said, "I received one morning a message from poor Goldsmith that he was in great distress, and as it was not in his power to come to me, begging that I would come to him as soon as possible. I sent him a guinea and promised to come to him directly. I accordingly went as soon as I was drest, and found that his landlady had arrested him for his rent, at which he was in a violent passion. I perceived that he had already changed my guinea, and had got a bottle of Madeira and a glass before him. I put the cork into the bottle, desired he would be calm, and began to talk to him of the means by which he might be extricated. He then told me that he had a novel ready for the press, which he produced to me. I looked into it, and saw its merit; told the landlady I should soon return, and having gone to a bookseller sold it for sixty pounds. I brought Goldsmith the money and he discharged his rent, not without rating his landlady in a high tone for having used him so ill."

Investigation of old account books of the publisher Newbery shows that in October, 1762, Goldsmith himself sold a printer, Benjamin Collins, a third share of the story.

This seems at first contradictory of Johnson's story. But Mr. Dobson suggests that Johnson probably went to Newbery or Strahan and "settled upon the price of the manuscript, and procured for Goldsmith 'immediate relief' in the shape of an advance for one or for two shares. The other share or shares would remain to be disposed of by the author." The question has also been raised as to why the publication of the story was so long delayed. The usual explanation, following Johnson's suggestions to that effect, is that the publisher "had such faint hopes of its success that he did not publish it till after *The Traveller* so increased its author's fame." This is hardly tenable, because *The Traveller* had been published eight months before *The Vicar of Wakefield* appeared. It is more likely, as Mr. Dobson points out, that the story was practically finished when Johnson used it to relieve Goldsmith's necessities, and then the author, with characteristic procrastination, delayed to put it in final form.

Had Goldsmith lived half a century earlier, instead of the story of *The Vicar of Wakefield*, we should probably have had the Primrose family immortalized in a charming series of papers, on the order of the *De Coverley* papers of Addison. The characterization of the good doctor and his wife is natural and charming, the sketches and descriptions are inimitable in their grace and genial humor. Because Richardson, Fielding, and Smollett, the fathers of the English novel, had lately made story-telling popular, Goldsmith tried to throw his material into the form of a novel.

The Vicar of Wakefield was published in March, 1766. The periodicals of the day had little to say about it. Some did not mention it at all, those that did confined themselves to a bare recital of the plot. The book was left to the public, but fortunately the public was at no loss as to its verdict. The book took its place as a classic, a masterpiece of English letters, — a place which has never been disputed.

Goldsmith, his sixty guineas for *The Vicar of Wakefield* out of hand almost before it was in hand, continued hack work. He often undertook to write about subjects of which he knew little, and he had neither time nor inclination for learned research, but his clear narrative and graceful style made his compilations readable and salable.

Goldsmith had always been a lover of the stage, and in 1766 he wrote a play, *The Good-natured Man*. After many delays and difficulties, it was put on the stage. Owing largely to the jealousy and rivalry of Garrick, it was not a stage success; but it was a financial success, bringing the author about five hundred pounds. This seemed a mine of wealth to the improvident Goldsmith. He indulged his passion for fine clothes, swaggering in plum-colored velvet and scarlet silks on the street where he had run errands ten years before as a ragged clerk. Concerning the "heedless expenses" of this time, Irving says very justly: "The debts which he thus thoughtlessly incurred in consequence of a transient gleam of prosperity embarrassed him for the rest of his life; so that the success of *The Good-natured Man* may be said to have been ruinous to him."

He moved into more commodious and more expensive rooms in the Temple, — "two reasonably sized, old fashioned rooms, with a third smaller room, or sleeping closet." These he furnished handsomely, and here he made merry with a round of suppers and dinners, card and tea parties. He was always ready to sing an Irish song or to join the young people, whom he loved to entertain in a game of blindman's buff. The grave lawyer Blackstone had the rooms below and was busy writing his *Commentaries*.

Often and often was he disturbed in his work by the romps and frolics above.

The summer of 1768 was saddened for Goldsmith by tidings of the death of his beloved brother Henry. He was now composing a descriptive poem, full of reminiscences of home and childhood. The memory of his dear brother was with him as he strolled about the lanes and fields of the quiet country place where he had taken refuge, and it inspired some of the noblest passages of *The Deserted Village*, — for the character of the village preacher is said to embody Goldsmith's recollections of his father and his brother, who inherited his character and adopted his father's profession. The character of the village schoolmaster is drawn from Goldsmith's early master, Thomas Byrne. The poem, which he dedicated to Sir Joshua Reynolds, was not published until May, 1770. A friend says, "Goldsmith, though quick enough at prose, was rather slow in his poetry, — not from the tardiness of fancy, but from the time he took in pointing the sentiment and polishing the versification." He made a first draft with lines far apart, and so interlined and rewrote that hardly a line remained in its original form. All the labor on *The Deserted Village* was well spent in polishing the gem to take its place among the treasures of the English language. It is said that Goldsmith received a hundred guineas for this poem. It is said, furthermore, that some one remarked to him that this was a great price for so small a poem.

"In truth," said Goldsmith, "I think so too; it is much more than the honest man can afford or the piece is worth. I have not been easy since I received it."

Forthwith he returned the money to the bookseller, leaving the poem to be paid for according to its success.

While *The Deserted Village* was on hand, Goldsmith's

pen was busy with the usual treatises and abridgments. He followed a *Roman History* with a *History of Animated Nature* in eight volumes, and an *English History* in four. Though he had to take his information on natural history at second hand, the "good sense and the delightful simplicity of its style" made his book more readable than others of greater depth and scope. Dr. Johnson said, "He has the art of compiling and of saying everything he has to say in a pleasing manner. He is now writing a *Natural History*, and will make it as entertaining as a Persian tale."

In 1769 the King appointed Goldsmith Professor of Ancient History to the Royal Academy and Johnson Professor of Ancient Literature.

A few weeks after the publication of *The Deserted Village*, Goldsmith made a holiday excursion to Paris with a friend, Mrs. Horneck, and her two beautiful daughters. He did not enjoy as much as he had anticipated his visit to the scenes he had visited as a vagabond of twenty, traveling on foot, trusting to his flute and the good nature of peasants for food and lodging. Now he was a fashionable idler, with a carriage, a wig, a velvet suit — and forty years. He was glad to return to London even to the hack work which his reckless expenditures made necessary. He prepared an abridgment of his *Roman History* and a *Life of Bolingbroke*. One of his infrequent poems, the amusing *Haunch of Venison*, was called forth by a present of game from his friend Lord Clare.

About this time he wrote another comedy, *She Stoops to Conquer; or, The Mistakes of a Night*, the plot of which turns on an incident in his own life which has already been told. The play was accepted, but lay for months in the hands of Colman, the stage manager, who predicted its failure. Its financial success was a matter of even greater moment to poor debt-burdened Goldsmith than its literary success. On the fateful night when it was acted for the first time he walked the streets in an agony of suspense and foreboding. At last he mustered courage to go to the theater, where Johnson and his stanch friends had assembled to give the play their countenance and applause. They were not needed. The merits of the play — its natural dialogue, its clever characterizations, its genial humor and wit — won the day. It was a pronounced success from the first, and it holds its place on the stage to-day as one of the finest English comedies.

"I know of no comedy for many years that has so much exhilarated an audience; that has answered so much the great end of comedy — making an audience merry," said Dr. Johnson.

The play was published immediately and was justly dedicated to Dr. Johnson, who took a protecting, almost fatherly, interest in Goldsmith's affairs. In financial matters the play afforded Goldsmith little more than temporary relief. He had already received from the publishers more than they agreed to pay for it, and the four or five hundred pounds of stage profits passed quickly through his fingers. He wrote a *Grecian History* on the plan of his *Roman History*, and of this, too, the money was spent before it was earned. He planned a great *Dictionary of Arts and Sciences*, to be edited by him with contributions from his friends, Johnson, Burke, Reynolds, and others, but he could not find a publisher to support the scheme.

His last years were darkened with cares, failing health, and pecuniary embarrassments. But his genial wit and humor shone out, a light in the darkness. On one occasion, when he came late to a literary dinner, the guests fell into the whim of writing mock epitaphs upon him.

His ugly face, his clumsy figure, absurd in satin and velvet, his simple vanity and credulity, his impudence of shyness and embarrassment — these peculiarities and frailties lent themselves readily to satire and were dealt with ungently by the assembled wits. The most famous of these epitaphs was composed by Garrick : —

> "Here lies poet Goldsmith for shortness called Noll,
> Who wrote like an angel but talked like poor Poll."

Wisely trusting repartee to his pen rather than to his tongue, Goldsmith answered in the poem called *Retaliation: Including Epitaphs on the most Distinguished Wits of the Metropolis.* This "incomparable series of epigrammatic portraits which is to-day one of the most graphic picture galleries of his immediate contemporaries" was written only a few days before Goldsmith's death. When it was published the author was no more.

He had been in feeble health for months, and was finally prostrated by a low fever. His physician said, "You are worse than you should be from the degree of fever which you have. Is your mind at ease?"

"No, it is not," answered poor Goldsmith. These were his last words. On the morning of April 4, 1774, he died. The tidings of the gentle humorist's death brought grief to many a heart. Burke burst into tears, Reynolds laid aside his pencil, Johnson was plunged in gloom. The stairs were crowded with humble mourners, men and women and children, the afflicted and the infirm, who wept the loss of their friend.

"Let not his frailties be remembered," wrote Johnson; "he was a very great man." He is indeed one of the foremost figures of a brilliant age. *The Citizen of the World, The Deserted Village, She Stoops to Conquer,* and *The Vicar of Wakefield* rank among the masterpieces of English literature, and confer on their author the distinction of having excelled as essayist, as poet, as playwright, and as novelist.

A monument to Goldsmith was erected in Westminster Abbey, on which was set forth in a Latin inscription, by Dr. Johnson, that it was to the memory "of Oliver Goldsmith, a poet, naturalist, historian, who left hardly any style of writing untouched, and touched nothing that he did not adorn; of all the passions, whether smiles were to be moved or tears, a powerful yet gentle master; in genius sublime, vivid, versatile; in style elevated, clear, elegant."

CRITICAL OPINIONS

THERE have been many greater writers, but perhaps no writer was ever more uniformly agreeable. His style was always pure and easy, and, on proper occasions, pointed and energetic. His narratives were always amusing, his descriptions always picturesque, his humor rich and joyous, yet not without an occasional tinge of amiable sadness. About everything that he wrote, serious or sportive, there was a certain natural grace and decorum. . . . There was in his character much to love, but very little to respect. His heart was soft even to weakness; he was so generous that he quite forgot to be just; he forgave injuries so readily that he might be said to invite them; and was so liberal to beggars that he had nothing left for his tailor and his butcher. — *T. B. Macaulay.*

While the productions of writers of loftier pretension and more sounding names are suffered to molder on our shelves, those of Goldsmith are cherished and laid in our bosoms. We do not quote them with ostentation, but they mingle with our minds, sweeten our tempers, and harmonize our thoughts; they put us in good humor with ourselves and with the world, and in so doing they make us happier and better. — *Washington Irving.*

It would be easy to multiply examples of that strange mingling of strength and weakness — of genius and *gaucherie* — which went to make up Goldsmith's character.

Yet the advantage would remain with its gentler and more
lovable aspects, and the "over-word" would still be the
compassionate verdict: "Let not his frailties be remem-
bered, for he was a very great man." And . . . he was as-
suredly a great writer. In the fifteen years over which his
literary activity extended, he managed to produce a
record which has given him an unassailable place in Eng-
lish letters. Apart from mere hack work and compilation
— hack work and compilation which, in most cases, he all
but lifted to the level of a fine art — he wrote some of the
best familiar verse in the language. In an age barren of
poetry, he wrote two didactic poems, which are still among
the memories of old, as they are among the first lessons of
the young. He wrote a series of essays, which, for style
and individuality, fairly hold their own between the best
work of Addison and Steele on the one hand, and the best
work of Charles Lamb on the other. He wrote a domestic
novel, unique in kind, and as cosmopolitan as *Robinson
Crusoe*. Finally, he wrote two excellent plays, one of
which, *She Stoops to Conquer*, still stands in the front rank
of the few popular masterpieces of English comedy.

— *Austin Dobson.*

Who of the millions whom he has amused does not love
him? To be the most beloved of English writers — what a
title that is for a man! A wild youth, wayward but full
of tenderness and affection, quits the country village where
his boyhood had been passed in happy musing, in idle
shelter, in fond longing to see the great world out of doors,
and achieve name and fortune — and after years of dire
struggle and neglect and poverty, his heart turning back
as fondly to his native place as it had longed eagerly for
change when sheltered there, he writes a book and a poem,
full of the recollections and feelings of home — he paints

the fields and scenes of his youth, and peoples Auburn and Wakefield with remembrances of Lissoy. Wander he must, but he carries away a home relic with him, and dies with it on his breast. His nature is truant; in repose it longs for change, as on the journey it looks back for friends and quiet. He passes to-day in building an air-castle for to-morrow, or in writing yesterday's elegy; and he would fly away this hour but that a cage necessity keeps him. What is the charm of his verse, of his style, and humor, his sweet regrets, his delicate compassion, his soft smile, his tremulous sympathy, the weakness which he owns? Your love for him is half pity. You come hot and tired from the day's battle and this sweet minstrel sings to you. Who could harm the kind vagrant harper? Whom did he ever hurt? He carries no weapon — save the box on which he plays to you; and with which he delights great and humble, young and old, the captains in the tents, or the soldiers round the fire, or the women and children in the villages, at whose porches he stops and sings his simple songs of love and beauty. With that sweet story of *The Vicar of Wakefield* he has found entry into every castle and every hamlet in Europe. Not one of us, however busy or hard, but once or twice in our lives has passed an evening with him and undergone the charm of his delightful music. — *W. M. Thackeray.*

CRITICAL ESTIMATES

It would be difficult to point out one among the English poets less likely to be excelled in his own style than the author of *The Deserted Village*. Possessing much of Pope's versification without the monotonous structure of his line; rising sometimes to the swell and fulness of Dryden without his inflation; delicate and masterly in his description; graceful in one of the greatest graces of poetry, its transitions; alike successful in his sportive or grave, his playful or melancholy mood; he may long bid defiance to the numerous competitors whom the friendship or flattery of the present age is so hastily arraying against him. — *Sir Walter Scott.*

Goldsmith being mentioned, Johnson observed that it was long before his merit came to be acknowledged; that he once complained to him, in ludicrous terms of distress, "Whenever I write anything, the public *make a point* to know nothing about it"; but that his *Traveler* brought him into high reputation. Langton: There is not one bad line in that poem; not one of Dryden's careless verses. Sir Joshua: I was glad to hear Charles Fox say, it was one of the finest poems in the English language. Langton: Why was you glad? You surely had no doubt of this before? Johnson: No, the merit of *The Traveler* is so well established, that Mr. Fox's praise cannot augment it nor his censure diminish it. Sir Joshua: But his friends may suspect that they had too great partiality for him. Johnson: Nay, sir, the partiality of his friends was always against him. It was with difficulty we could give him a hearing. — *Boswell's Life of Johnson.*

The execution [of *The Traveler*], though deserving of much praise, is far inferior to the design. No philosophic poem, ancient or modern, has a plan so noble and at the same time so simple. An English wanderer, seated on a crag among the Alps, near the point where three great countries meet, looks down on the boundless prospect, reviews his long pilgrimage, recalls the varieties of scenery, of climate, of government, of religion, of national character, which he has observed, and comes to the conclusion, just or unjust, that our happiness depends little on political institutions, and much on the temper and regulation of our minds. — *Macaulay*.

A little poem which we passionately received into our circle allowed us from henceforward to think of nothing else. Goldsmith's *Deserted Village* necessarily delighted every one at that grade of cultivation, in that sphere of thought. Not as living and active, but as a departed, vanished existence, was described, all that one so readily looked upon, that one loved, prized, sought passionately in the present, to take part in it with the cheerfulness of youth. . . . Here, again, we found an honest Wakefield, in his well-known circle, yet no longer in his living, bodily form, but as a shadow recalled by the soft, mournful tones of the elegiac poet. The very thought of this picture is one of the happiest possible, when once the design is formed to evoke once more an innocent past with a graceful melancholy. And in this kindly endeavor, how well has the Englishman succeeded in every sense of the word! — *Goethe*.

We do not read *The Deserted Village* for its political economy: we read it for its idyllic sweetness; for its portraits of the village preacher, of the village schoolmaster, of the country inn; for its pathetic description of the poor

emigrants; for the tender and noble feeling with which
Goldsmith closes the poem in his farewell to poetry
                                                    — *L. Du Pont Syle.*

At most we can allow it [*The Hermit*] accomplishment
and ease.   But its sweetness has grown a little insipid,
and its simplicity, to eyes unanointed with eighteenth-
century sympathy, borders perilously upon the ludicrous.
                                                    — *Austin Dobson.*

The characters of his distinguished intimates are ad-
mirably hit off [in *Retaliation*], with a mixture of generous
praise and good-humored raillery.   In fact, the poem, for
its graphic truth, its nice discrimination, its terse good
sense, and its shrewd knowledge of the world, must have
electrified the club almost as much as the first appearance
of *The Traveler*, and let them still deeper into the charac-
ter and talents of the man they had been accustomed to
consider as their butt.   *Retaliation*, in a word, closed his
accounts with the club, and balanced all his previous
deficiencies. — *Washington Irving.*

Retaliation is the most mischievous and the most play-
ful, the friendliest and the faithfulest of satires.   How
much better we know Garrick because Goldsmith has
shown him to us in his acting off the stage!   And do we
as often think of Reynolds in any attitude as in that of
smiling non-listener to the critical coxcombs?

"When they talked of their Raphaels, Correggios, and
       stuff,
He shifted his trumpet and only took snuff."

Would that the portraits of Johnson and of Boswell had
been added. — *Edward Dowden.*

BIBLIOGRAPHY

Life of Oliver Goldsmith : James Prior.
Life and Times of Goldsmith : John Forster.
Goldsmith : William Black.
The Life of Oliver Goldsmith : Washington Irving.
Sterne and Goldsmith (English Humourists): W. M. Thackeray.
Life of Oliver Goldsmith : Austin Dobson.
Life of Samuel Johnson : James Boswell.
The Vicar of Wakefield : Parchment edition, with preface and
    notes by Austin Dobson.   Kegan Paul, Trench & Co.
The Vicar of Wakefield : Bohn's Standard Library.   George
    Bell & Sons.

An exhaustive bibliography is appended to Austin Dobson's
authoritative Life of Goldsmith.

CHRONOLOGY

Goldsmith	English Literature	History
Nov. 10, 1728. Born at Pallas, Ireland.	1726–30. Thomson's "Seasons."	1733. Settlement of Georgia.
1730. Removed to Lissoy.	1736. Butler's "Analogy."	1739–48. The Spanish War.
	1741. Richardson's "Pamela."	
	1742–4. Young's "Night Thoughts."	
	1744. Akenside's "Pleasures of the Imagination."	1744–8. King George's War.
		1746. The young Pretender defeated at Culloden.
1748. Entered Trinity College, Dublin.	1746. Collins's "Odes."	1748. Treaty of Aix-la-Chapelle.
Feb. 27, 1749. Left Dublin, with degree of B.A.	1749. Fielding's "Tom Jones."	
1752. Went to Edinburgh to study medicine.	1750. Johnson's "Rambler."	
	1751. Gray's "Elegy."	
1754. Went to Leyden.	1753–61. Hume's "History of England."	
1755–6. Traveled in Germany, France, Switzerland, and Italy.		1755. French and Indian War.
1756. Returned to England; went to London.	1756. Burke's "Enquiry on the Sublime and the Beautiful."	1756–63. Seven Years' War.
	1757. Gray's "Odes."	
1759. Enquiry into the State of Polite Learning in Europe.	1758. Johnson's "Idler," "Rasselas."	1759. English Conquest of Canada.

1760. Chinese Letters.	1760. Sterne's "Tristram Shandy."	1760. Accession of George III.
1761. Moved to Wine Office Court; made Johnson's acquaintance.		
1762. Citizen of the World (Chinese Letters).		1763. Peace of Paris.
1763. Elected a member of "The Club."		1765. Passage of Stamp Act.
1764. The Traveller; History of England in a series of letters.		
1765. Essays.		1766. Repeal of Stamp Act.
1766. The Vicar of Wakefield.	1768. Sterne's "Sentimental Journey." Death of Sterne.	1768. Royal Academy founded.
1768. The Good-natured Man; appointed Professor of Ancient History in the Royal Academy.		
1769. Roman History.	1770. Burke's "Present Discontents."	1770. Boston Massacre.
1770. The Deserted Village; visited Paris.	1771. Smollett's "Humphrey Clinker." Death of Smollett.	
1771. History of England.		
1773. She Stoops to Conquer.		1774. Death of Louis XV. of France.
1774. Grecian History; History of the Earth and Animated Nature; Retaliation, unfinished; April 4, died in London.		

DEDICATION

TO THE REV. HENRY GOLDSMITH

Dear Sir,

I am sensible that the friendship between us can acquire no new force from the ceremonies of a dedication; and perhaps it demands an excuse thus to prefix your name to my attempts, which you decline giving with your own. But as a part of this poem was formerly written to you from Switzerland, the whole can now, with propriety, be only inscribed to you. It will also throw a light upon many parts of it, when the reader understands that it is addressed to a man who, despising fame and fortune, has retired early to happiness and obscurity, with an income of forty pounds a year.

I now perceive, my dear brother, the wisdom of your humble choice. You have entered upon a sacred office, where the harvest is great, and the laborers are but few; while you have left the field of ambition, where the laborers are many, and the harvest not worth carrying away. But of all kinds of ambition, — what from the refinement of the times, from different systems of criticisms, and from the divisions of party, — that which pursues poetical fame is the wildest.

Poetry makes a principal amusement among unpolished nations; but in a country verging to the extremes of refinement, painting and music come in for a share. As these offer the feeble mind a less laborious entertainment, they at first rival poetry, and at length supplant her; they engross all that favor once shown to her, and though but younger sisters, seize upon the elder's birthright.

Yet, however this art may be neglected by the powerful, it is still in greater danger from the mistaken efforts of the learned to improve it. What criticisms have we not heard of late in favor of blank verse, and Pindaric odes, choruses, anapests and iambics, alliterative care and happy negligence! Every absurdity has now a champion to defend it; and as he is generally much in the wrong, so he has always much to say; for error is ever talkative.

But there is an enemy to this art still more dangerous, I mean Party. Party entirely distorts the judgment, and destroys the taste. When the mind is once infected with this disease, it can only find pleasure in what contributes to increase the distemper. Like the tiger, that seldom desists from pursuing man after having once preyed upon human flesh, the reader, who has once gratified his appetite with calumny, makes, ever after, the most agreeable feast upon murdered reputation. Such readers generally admire some half-witted thing, who wants to be thought a bold man, having lost the character of a wise one. Him they dignify with the name of poet; his tawdry lampoons are called satires, his turbulence is said to be force, and his frenzy fire.

What reception a poem may find, which has neither abuse, party, nor blank verse to support it, I cannot tell, nor am I solicitous to know. My aims are right. Without espousing the cause of any party, I have attempted to moderate the rage of all. I have endeavored to show, that there may be equal happiness in states that are differently governed from our own; that every state has a particular principle of happiness, and that this principle in each may be carried to a mischievous excess. There are few can judge, better than yourself, how far these positions are illustrated in this poem.

I am, dear Sir,

Your most affectionate Brother,

OLIVER GOLDSMITH.

THE TRAVELER

OR, A PROSPECT OF SOCIETY

REMOTE, unfriended, melancholy, slow,
Or by the lazy Scheld or wandering Po;
Or onward, where the rude Carinthian boor
Against the houseless stranger shuts the door;
Or where Campania's plain forsaken lies,   5
A weary waste expanding to the skies;
Where'er I roam, whatever realms to see,
My heart untravel'd fondly turns to thee;
Still to my brother turns, with ceaseless pain,
And drags at each remove a lengthening chain. 10
   Eternal blessings crown my earliest friend,
And round his dwelling guardian saints attend:
Blest be that spot where cheerful guests retire
To pause from toil, and trim their ev'ning fire:
Blest that abode where want and pain repair, 15
And every stranger finds a ready chair:
Blest be those feasts, with simple plenty crown'd,
Where all the ruddy family around
Laugh at the jests or pranks that never fail,

20 Or sigh with pity at some mournful tale;
Or press the bashful stranger to his food,
And learn the luxury of doing good.
    But me, not destin'd such delights to share,
My prime of life in wand'ring spent and care;
25 Impell'd, with steps unceasing, to pursue
Some fleeting good that mocks me with the
        view;
That, like the circle bounding earth and skies,
Allures from far, yet, as I follow, flies;
My fortune leads to traverse realms alone,
30 And find no spot of all the world my own.
    Even now, where Alpine solitudes ascend,
I sit me down a pensive hour to spend;
And plac'd on high above the storm's career,
Look downward where an hundred realms
        appear;
35 Lakes, forests, cities, plains extending wide,
The pomp of kings, the shepherd's humbler
        pride.
    When thus Creation's charms around com-
        bine,
Amidst the store should thankless pride re-
        pine?

Say, should the philosophic mind disdain
That good which makes each humbler bosom vain?
Let school-taught pride dissemble all it can, 41
These little things are great to little man;
And wiser he, whose sympathetic mind
Exults in all the good of all mankind.
Ye glitt'ring towns, with wealth and splendor
      crown'd; 45
Ye fields, where summer spreads profusion round;
Ye lakes, whose vessels catch the busy gale;
Ye bending swains, that dress the flow'ry vale;
For me your tributary stores combine:
Creation's heir, the world, the world is mine. 50
  As some lone miser, visiting his store,
Bends at his treasure, counts, recounts it o'er;
Hoards after hoards his rising raptures fill,
Yet still he sighs, for hoards are wanting still:
Thus to my breast alternate passions rise, 55
Pleas'd with each good that Heaven to man
      supplies:
Yet oft a sigh prevails, and sorrows fall,
To see the hoard of human bliss so small;
And oft I wish amidst the scene to find
Some spot to real happiness consign'd, 60

Where my worn soul, each wand'ring hope at
    rest,
May gather bliss to see my fellows blest.
    But where to find that happiest spot below
Who can direct, when all pretend to know?
65 The shudd'ring tenant of the frigid zone
Boldly proclaims that happiest spot his own;
Extols the treasures of his stormy seas,
And his long nights of revelry and ease:
The naked negro, panting at the line,
70 Boasts of his golden sands and palmy wine,
Basks in the glare, or stems the tepid wave,
And thanks his gods for all the good they gave.
Such is the patriot's boast where'er we roam;
His first, best country ever is at home.
75 And yet, perhaps, if countries we compare,
And estimate the blessings which they share,
Tho' patriots flatter, still shall wisdom find
An equal portion dealt to all mankind;
As different good, by Art or Nature given,
80 To different nations makes their blessings
    even.
    Nature, a mother kind alike to all,
Still grants her bliss at Labor's earnest call:

With food as well the peasant is supply'd
On Idra's cliffs as Arno's shelvy side;
And though the rocky crested summits frown,   85
These rocks by custom turn to beds of down.
From Art more various are the blessings sent;
Wealth, commerce, honor, liberty, content.
Yet these each other's power so strong contest,
That either seems destructive of the rest.   90
Where wealth and freedom reign, contentment fails
And honor sinks where commerce long prevails.
Hence every state, to one lov'd blessing prone,
Conforms and models life to that alone.
Each to the favorite happiness attends,   95
And spurns the plan that aims at other ends:
Till carried to excess in each domain,
This fav'rite good begets peculiar pain.
    But let us try these truths with closer eyes,
And trace them through the prospect as it lies: 100
Here for a while my proper cares resign'd,
Here let me sit in sorrow for mankind;
Like yon neglected shrub at random cast,
That shades the steep, and sighs at every blast.
    Far to the right, where Apennine ascends,   105
Bright as the summer, Italy extends:

Its uplands sloping deck the mountain's side,
Woods over woods in gay theatric pride;
While oft some temple's mould'ring tops be-
    tween
110 With venerable grandeur mark the scene.
Could Nature's bounty satisfy the breast,
The sons of Italy were surely blest.
Whatever fruits in different climes were found,
That proudly rise, or humbly court the ground;
115 Whatever blooms in torrid tracts appear,
Whose bright succession decks the varied
    year;
Whatever sweets salute the northern sky
With vernal lives, that blossom but to die;
These, here disporting, own the kindred soil,
120 Nor ask luxuriance from the planter's toil;
While sea-born gales their gelid wings expand
To winnow fragrance round the smiling land.
But small the bliss that sense alone bestows,
And sensual bliss is all the nation knows.
125 In florid beauty groves and fields appear;
Man seems the only growth that dwindles here.
Contrasted faults through all his manners
    reign:

Though poor, luxurious; though submissive, vain;
Though grave, yet trifling; zealous, yet untrue;
And ev'n in penance planning sins anew. 130
All evils here contaminate the mind
That opulence departed leaves behind;
For wealth was theirs, not far remov'd the date
When commerce proudly flourish'd· through the
    state;
At her command the palace learnt to rise, 135
Again the long-fallen column sought the skies,
The canvas glow'd, beyond e'en nature warm,
The pregnant quarry teem'd with human form;
Till, more unsteady than the southern gale,
Commerce on other shores display'd her sail; 140
While nought remain'd of all that riches gave,
But towns unman'd, and lords without a slave:
And late the nation found with fruitless skill
Its former strength was but plethoric ill.
    Yet still the loss of wealth is here supplied 145
By arts, the splendid wrecks of former pride;
From these the feeble heart and long-fall'n mind
An easy compensation seem to find.
Here may be seen, in bloodless pomp array'd,
The paste-board triumph and the cavalcade, 150

Processions form'd for piety and love,
A mistress or a saint in every grove.
By sports like these are all their cares beguil'd;
The sports of children satisfy the child.
155 Each nobler aim, represt by long control,
Now sinks at last, or feebly mans the soul;
While low delights, succeeding fast behind,
In happier meanness occupy the mind:
As in those domes where Cæsars once bore
    sway,
160 Defac'd by time and tottering in decay,
There in the ruin, heedless of the dead,
The shelter-seeking peasant builds his shed;
And, wond'ring man could want the larger pile,
Exults, and owns his cottage with a smile.
165   My soul, turn from them, turn we to survey,
Where rougher climes a nobler race display;
Where the bleak Swiss their stormy mansions
    tread,
And force a churlish soil for scanty bread.
No product here the barren hills afford,
170 But man and steel, the soldier and his sword:
No vernal blooms their torpid rocks array,
But winter ling'ring chills the lap of May:

No Zephyr fondly sues the mountain's breast,
But meteors glare, and stormy glooms invest.
  Yet, still, even here content can spread a charm,
Redress the clime, and all its rage disarm.   176
Though poor the peasant's hut, his feasts tho'
    small,
He sees his little lot the lot of all;
Sees no contiguous palace rear its head
To shame the meanness of his humble shed;   180
No costly lord the sumptuous banquet deal
To make him loath his vegetable meal;
But calm, and bred in ignorance and toil,
Each wish contracting fits him to the soil.
Cheerful at morn he wakes from short repose,   185
Breathes the keen air, and carols as he goes;
With patient angle trolls the finny deep;
Or drives his venturous plow-share to the steep;
Or seeks the den where snow-tracks mark the way,
And drags the struggling savage into day.   190
At night returning, every labor sped,
He sits him down the monarch of a shed;
Smiles by his cheerful fire, and round surveys
His children's looks, that brighten at the blaze;
While his lov'd partner, boastful of her hoard, 195

Displays her cleanly platter on the board:
And haply too some pilgrim, thither led,
With many a tale repays the nightly bed.

Thus every good his native wilds impart
200 Imprints the patriot passion on his heart;
And e'en those ills that round his mansion rise
Enhance the bliss his scanty fund supplies.
Dear is that shed to which his soul conforms,
And dear that hill which lifts him to the
     storms;
205 And as a child, when scaring sounds molest,
Clings close and closer to the mother's breast,
So the loud torrent and the whirlwind's roar
But bind him to his native mountains more.

Such are the charms to barren states as-
     sign'd;
210 Their wants but few, their wishes all confin'd.
Yet let them only share the praises due:
If few their wants, their pleasures are but few;
For every want that stimulates the breast
Becomes a source of pleasure when redrest;
215 Whence from such lands each pleasing science
     flies
That first excites desire, and then supplies;

Unknown to them, when sensual pleasures cloy,
To fill the languid pause with finer joy;
Unknown those powers that raise the soul to flame,
Catch every nerve, and vibrate through the frame.
Their level life is but a smold'ring fire, 221
Unquench'd by want, unfann'd by strong desire;
Unfit for raptures, or, if raptures cheer
On some high festival of once a year,
In wild excess the vulgar breast takes fire, 225
Till, buried in debauch, the bliss expire.

 But not their joys alone thus coarsely flow:
Their morals, like their pleasures, are but low;
For, as refinement stops, from sire to son
Unalter'd, unimprov'd, the manners run, 230
And love's and friendship's finely-pointed dart
Fall blunted from each indurated heart.
Some sterner virtues o'er the mountain's breast
May sit, like falcons, cow'ring on the nest;
But all the gentler morals, such as play 235
Thro' life's more cultur'd walks, and charm the
  way,
These, far dispers'd, on timorous pinions fly,
To sport and flutter in a kinder sky.

 To kinder skies, where gentler manners **reign,**

240 I turn; and France displays her bright domain.
   Gay, sprightly land of mirth and social ease,
   Pleas'd with thyself, whom all the world can
      please,
   How often have I led thy sportive choir,
   With tuneless pipe, beside the murmuring
      Loire?
245 Where shading elms along the margin grew,
   And freshen'd from the wave the Zephyr flew;
   And haply, though my harsh touch, faltering
      still,
   But mocked all tune, and marr'd the dancer's
      skill,
   Yet would the village praise my wonderous
      power,
250 And dance, forgetful of the noon-tide hour.
   Alike all ages. Dames of ancient days
   Have led their children through the mirthful
      maze,
   And the gay grandsire, skill'd in gestic lore,
   Has frisk'd beneath the burthen of threescore.
255   So blest a life these thoughtless realms
      display;
   Thus idly busy rolls their world away;

Theirs are those arts that mind to mind endear,
For honor forms the social temper here.
Honor, that praise which real merit gains,
Or even imaginary worth obtains, 260
Here passes current: paid from hand to hand,
It shifts in splendid traffic round the land;
From courts to camps, to cottages, it strays,
And all are taught an avarice of praise.
They please, are pleas'd; they give to get esteem;
Till, seeming blest, they grow to what they seem.
But while this softer art their bliss supplies, 267
It gives their follies also room to rise;
For praise too dearly lov'd, or warmly sought,
Enfeebles all internal strength of thought, 270
And the weak soul, within itself unblest,
Leans for all pleasure on another's breast.
Hence ostentation here, with tawdry art,
Pants for the vulgar praise which fools impart;
Here vanity assumes her pert grimace, 275
And trims her robes of frieze with copper lace;
Here beggar pride defrauds her daily cheer,
To boast one splendid banquet once a year;
The mind still turns where shifting fashion draws,
Nor weighs the solid worth of self-applause. 280

To men of other minds my fancy flies,
Embosom'd in the deep where Holland lies.
Methinks her patient sons before me stand,
Where the broad ocean leans against the land,
285 And, sedulous to stop the coming tide,
Lift the tall rampire's artificial pride.
Onward methinks, and diligently slow,
The firm connected bulwark seems to grow;
Spreads its long arms amidst the watry roar,
290 Scoops out an empire, and usurps the shore.
While the pent ocean, rising o'er the pile,
Sees an amphibious world beneath him smile:
The slow canal, the yellow blossom'd vale,
The willow tufted bank, the gliding sail,
295 The crowded mart, the cultivated plain, —
A new creation rescu'd from his reign.

    Thus while around the wave-subjected soil
Impels the native to repeated toil,
Industrious habits in each bosom reign,
300 And industry begets a love of gain.
Hence all the good from opulence that springs,
With all those ills superfluous treasure brings,
Are here display'd.   Their much-lov'd wealth
    imparts

Convenience, plenty, elegance, and arts:
But view them closer, craft and fraud appear; 305
E'en liberty itself is barter'd here.
At gold's superior charms all freedom flies;
The needy sell it, and the rich man buys;
A land of tyrants, and a den of slaves,
Here wretches seek dishonorable graves,   310
And calmly bent, to servitude conform,
Dull as their lakes that slumber in the storm.
  Heavens! how unlike their Belgic sires of old,
Rough, poor, content, ungovernably bold;
War in each breast, and freedom on each brow: 315
How much unlike the sons of Britain now!
  Fir'd at the sound, my genius spreads her wing,
And flies where Britain courts the western spring;
Where lawns extend that scorn Arcadian pride,
And brighter streams than fam'd Hydaspis glide.
There all around the gentlest breezes stray;   321
There gentle music melts on every spray;
Creation's mildest charms are there combin'd,
Extremes are only in the master's mind!
Stern o'er each bosom Reason holds her state, 325
With daring aims irregularly great;
Pride in their port, defiance in their eye,

I see the lords of human kind pass by;
Intent on high designs, a thoughtful band,
330 By forms unfashion'd, fresh from Nature's
        hand,
Fierce in their native hardiness of soul,
True to imagin'd right, above control,
While even the peasant boasts these rights to
        scan,
And learns to venerate himself as man.
335   Thine, Freedom, thine the blessings pic-
        tur'd here;
Thine are those charms that dazzle and en-
        dear:
Too blest indeed, were such without alloy:
But foster'd even by Freedom ills annoy:
That independence Britons prize too high
340 Keeps man from man, and breaks the social tie;
The self-dependent lordlings stand alone,
All claims that bind and sweeten life unknown.
Here, by the bonds of nature feebly held,
Minds combat minds, repelling and repell'd;
345 Ferments arise, imprison'd factions roar,
Represt ambition struggles round her shore,
Till, over-wrought, the general system feels

Its motions stop, or frenzy fire the wheels.
  Nor this the worst. As nature's ties decay,
As duty, love, and honor fail to sway,   350
Fictitious bonds, the bonds of wealth and law,
Still gather strength, and force unwilling awe.
Hence all obedience bows to these alone,
And talent sinks, and merit weeps unknown:
Till time may come, when, stript of all her charms,
The land of scholars and the nurse of arms,   356
Where noble stems transmit the patriot flame,
Where kings have toil'd and poets wrote for fame,
One sink of level avarice shall lie,
And scholars, soldiers, kings, unhonor'd die.   360
  Yet think not, thus when Freedom's ills I state,
I mean to flatter kings, or court the great:
Ye powers of truth that bid my soul aspire,
Far from my bosom drive the low desire.
And thou, fair Freedom, taught alike to feel   365
The rabble's rage and tyrant's angry steel;
Thou transitory flower, alike undone
By proud contempt or favor's fostering sun,
Still may thy blooms the changeful clime endure!
I only would repress them to secure: 370
For just experience tells, in every soil,

That those who think must govern those that
  toil;
And all that Freedom's highest aims can reach
Is but to lay proportion'd loads on each.
375 Hence, should one order disproportioned grow,
Its double weight must ruin all below.
  O then how blind to all that truth requires,
Who think it freedom when a part aspires!
Calm is my soul, nor apt to rise in arms,
380 Except when fast approaching danger warms;
But when contending chiefs blockade the
  throne,
Contracting regal power to stretch their own,
When I behold a factious band agree
To call it freedom when themselves are free,
385 Each wanton judge new penal statutes draw,
Laws grind the poor, and rich men rule the
  law,
The wealth of climes where savage nations
  roam
Pillag'd from slaves to purchase slaves at
  home,
Fear, pity, justice, indignation start,
390 Tear off reserve, and bare my swelling heart;

Till half a patriot, half a coward grown,
I fly from petty tyrants to the throne.

  Yes, brother, curse with me that baleful hour
When first ambition struck at regal power;
And thus polluting honor in its source,   395
Gave wealth to sway the mind with double
    force.
Have we not seen, round Britain's peopled shore,
Her useful sons exchanged for useless ore,
Seen all her triumphs but destruction haste,
Like flaring tapers brightening as they waste? 400
Seen opulence, her grandeur to maintain,
Lead stern depopulation in her train,
And over fields where scattered hamlets rose
In barren solitary pomp repose?
Have we not seen at pleasure's lordly call   405
The smiling long-frequented village fall?
Beheld the duteous son, the sire decay'd,
The modest matron, and the blushing maid,
Forc'd from their homes, a melancholy train,
To traverse climes beyond the western main; 410
Where wild Oswego spreads her swamps around,
And Niagara stuns with thund'ring sound?
  Even now, perhaps, as there some pilgrim strays

Through tangled forests and through danger-
   ous ways,
415 Where beasts with man divided empire claim,
And the brown Indian marks with murderous
   aim;
There, while above the giddy tempest flies,
And all around distressful yells arise,
The pensive exile, bending with his woe,
420 To stop too fearful, and too faint to go,
Casts a long look where England's glories
   shine,
And bids his bosom sympathize with mine.
   Vain, very vain, my weary search to find
That bliss which only centres in the mind:
425 Why have I stray'd from pleasure and repose,
To seek a good each government bestows?
In every government, though terrors reign,
Though tyrant kings or tyrant laws restrain,
How small, of all that human hearts endure,
430 That part which laws or king can cause or cure!
Still to ourselves in every place consigned,
Our own felicity we make or find:
With secret course, which no loud storms
   annoy,

Glides the smooth current of domestic joy.
The lifted ax, the agonizing wheel,   435
Luke's iron crown, and Damien's bed of steel,
To men remote from power but rarely known,
Leave reason, faith, and conscience all our own.

DEDICATION

TO SIR JOSHUA REYNOLDS

DEAR SIR,

I can have no expectations in an address of this kind, either to add to your reputation, or to establish my own. You can gain nothing from my admiration, as I am ignorant of that art in which you are said to excel; and I may lose much by the severity of your judgment, as few have a juster taste in poetry than you. Setting interest therefore aside, to which I never paid much attention, I must be indulged at present in following my affections. The only dedication I ever made was to my brother, because I loved him better than most other men. He is since dead. Permit me to inscribe this Poem to you.

How far you may be pleased with the versification and mere mechanical parts of this attempt, I do not pretend to enquire; but I know you will object (and indeed several of our best and wisest friends concur in the opinion) that the depopulation it deplores is no where to be seen, and the disorders it laments are only to be found in the poet's own imagination. To this I can scarcely make any other answer than that I sincerely believe what I have written; that I have taken all possible pains, in my country excursions, for these four or five years past, to be certain of what I allege; and that all my views and enquiries have led me to believe those miseries real, which I here attempt to display. But this is not the place to enter into an enquiry, whether the country be depopulating, or not; the discussion would take up much room, and I should prove myself, at best, an indifferent politician, to tire the

61

reader with a long preface, when I want his unfatigued attention to a long poem.

In regretting the depopulation of the country, I inveigh against the increase of our luxuries; and here also I expect the shout of modern politicians against me. For twenty or thirty years past, it has been the fashion to consider luxury as one of the greatest national advantages; and all the wisdom of antiquity in that particular, as erroneous. Still, however, I must remain a professed ancient on that head, and continue to think those luxuries prejudicial to states, by which so many vices are introduced, and so many kingdoms have been undone. Indeed so much has been poured out of late on the other side of the question, that, merely for the sake of novelty and variety, one would sometimes wish to be in the right.

I am, Dear Sir,

Your sincere friend, and ardent admirer,

OLIVER GOLDSMITH.

THE DESERTED VILLAGE

Sweet Auburn! loveliest village of the plain;
Where health and plenty cheered the laboring
    swain,
Where smiling spring its earliest visit paid,
And parting summer's lingering blooms delayed:
Dear lovely bowers of innocence and ease,   5
Seats of my youth, when every sport could please,
How often have I loitered o'er thy green,
Where humble happiness endeared each scene!
How often have I paused on every charm,
The sheltered cot, the cultivated farm,   10
The never-failing brook, the busy mill,
The decent church that topt the neighboring hill,
The hawthorn bush, with seats beneath the shade,
For talking age and whispering lovers made!
How often have I blest the coming day,   15
When toil remitting lent its turn to play,
And all the village train, from labor free,
Led up their sports beneath the spreading tree,
While many a pastime circled in the shade,

20 The young contending as the old surveyed;
    And many a gambol frolicked o'er the ground,
    And sleights of art and feats of strength went
        round.
    And still, as each repeated pleasure tired,
    Succeeding sports the mirthful band inspired;
25 The dancing pair that simply sought renown
    By holding out to tire each other down;
    The swain mistrustless of his smutted face,
    While secret laughter tittered round the place;
    The bashful virgin's side-long looks of love,
30 The matron's glance that would those looks
        reprove.
    These were thy charms, sweet village! sports
        like these,
    With sweet succession, taught even toil to
        please:
    These round thy bowers their cheerful influ-
        ence shed:
    These were thy charms — but all these charms
        are fled.
35   Sweet smiling village, loveliest of the lawn,
    Thy sports are fled, and all thy charms with-
        drawn;

Amidst thy bowers the tyrant's hand is seen,
And desolation saddens all thy green:
One only master grasps the whole domain,
And half a tillage stints thy smiling plain.   40
No more thy glassy brook reflects the day,
But, choked with sedges, works its weedy way:
Along thy glades, a solitary guest,
The hollow sounding bittern guards its nest;
Amidst thy desert walks the lapwing flies,   45
And tires their echoes with unvaried cries;
Sunk are thy bowers in shapeless ruin all,
And the long grass o'ertops the moldering wall;
And trembling, shrinking from the spoiler's hand,
Far, far away thy children leave the land.   50

Ill fares the land, to hastening ills a prey,
Where wealth accumulates, and men decay:
Princes and lords may flourish, or may fade;
A breath can make them, as a breath has made:
But a bold peasantry, their country's pride,   55
When once destroyed, can never be supplied.

A time there was, ere England's griefs began,
When every rood of ground maintained its man;
For him light labor spread her wholesome store,
Just gave what life required, but gave no more: 60

His best companions, innocence and health;
And his best riches, ignorance of wealth.
But times are altered; trade's unfeeling train
Usurp the land and dispossess the swain;
65 Along the lawn, where scattered hamlets rose,
Unwieldy wealth and cumbrous pomp repose,
And every want to opulence allied,
And every pang that folly pays to pride.
These gentle hours that plenty bade to bloom,
70 Those calm desires that asked but little room,
Those healthful sports that graced the peace-
      ful scene,
Lived in each look, and brightened all the
      green;
These, far departing, seek a kinder shore,
And rural mirth and manners are no more.
75   Sweet Auburn! parent of the blissful hour,
Thy glades forlorn confess the tyrant's power.
Here, as I take my solitary rounds
Amidst thy tangling walks and ruined grounds,
And, many a year elapsed, return to view
80 Where once the cottage stood, the hawthorn
      grew,
Remembrance wakes with all her busy train,

Swells at my breast, and turns the past to pain.
In all my wanderings round this world of care,
In all my griefs — and GOD has given my share —
I still had hopes, my latest hours to crown,   85
Amidst these humble bowers to lay me down;
To husband out life's taper at the close,
And keep the flame from wasting by repose:
I still had hopes, for pride attends us still,
Amidst the swains to show my book-learned
    skill,   90
Around my fire an evening group to draw,
And tell of all I felt, and all I saw;
And, as an hare whom hounds and horns pursue
Pants to the place from whence at first she flew,
I still had hopes, my long vexations past,   95
Here to return — and die at home at last.
  O blest retirement, friend to life's decline,
Retreats from care, that never must be mine,
How happy he who crowns in shades like these
A youth of labor with an age of ease;   100
Who quits a world where strong temptations try,
And, since 'tis hard to combat, learns to fly!
For him no wretches, born to work and weep,
Explore the mine, or tempt the dangerous deep;

105 No surly porter stands in guilty state,
    To spurn imploring famine from the gate;
    But on he moves to meet his latter end,
    Angels around befriending Virtue's friend;
    Bends to the grave with unperceived decay,
110 While resignation gently slopes the way;
    And, all his prospects brightening to the last,
    His heaven commences ere the world be past!
      Sweet was the sound, when oft at evening's
        close
    Up yonder hill the village murmur rose.
115 There, as I past with careless steps and slow,
    The mingling notes came softened from below;
    The swain responsive as the milk-maid sung,
    The sober herd that lowed to meet their young,
    The noisy geese that gabbled o'er the pool,
120 The playful children just let loose from school,
    The watch-dog's voice that bayed the whis-
        pering wind,
    And the loud laugh that spoke the vacant
        mind; —
    These all in sweet confusion sought the shade,
    And filled each pause the nightingale had
        made.

But now the sounds of population fail,   125
No cheerful murmurs fluctuate in the gale,
No busy steps the grass-grown foot-way tread,
For all the bloomy flush of life is fled.
All but yon widowed, solitary thing,
That feebly bends beside the plashy spring: 130
She, wretched matron, forced in age, for bread,
To strip the brook with mantling cresses spread,
To pick her wintry fagot from the thorn,
To seek her nightly shed, and weep till morn;
She only left of all the harmless train,   135
The sad historian of the pensive plain.

   Near yonder copse, where once the garden ·
    smiled,
And still where many a garden flower grows wild;
There, where a few torn shrubs the place disclose,
The village preacher's modest mansion rose.   140
A man he was to all the country dear,
And passing rich with forty pounds a year;
Remote from towns he ran his godly race,
Nor e'er had changed, nor wished to change his
    place;
Unpractised he to fawn, or seek for power,   145
By doctrines fashioned to the varying hour;

Far other aims his heart had learned to prize,
More skilled to raise the wretched than to
rise.
His house was known to all the vagrant train;
150 He chid their wanderings but relieved their
pain:
The long remembered beggar was his guest,
Whose beard descending swept his aged breast;
The ruined spendthrift, now no longer proud,
Claimed kindred there, and had his claims
allowed;
155 The broken soldier, kindly bade to stay,
Sat by his fire, and talked the night away,
Wept o'er his wounds or tales of sorrow done,
Shouldered his crutch and shewed how fields
were won.
Pleased with his guests, the good man learned
to glow,
160 And quite forgot their vices in their woe;
Careless their merits or their faults to scan,
His pity gave ere charity began.
Thus to relieve the wretched was his pride,
And e'en his failings leaned to Virtue's side;
165 But in his duty prompt at every call,

He watched and wept, he prayed and felt for all;
And, as a bird each fond endearment tries
To tempt its new-fledged offspring to the skies,
He tried each art, reproved each dull delay,
Allured to brighter worlds, and led the way. 170
  Beside the bed where parting life was laid,
And sorrow, guilt, and pain by turns dismayed,
The reverend champion stood. At his control
Despair and anguish fled the struggling soul;
Comfort came down the trembling wretch to
    raise, 175
And his last faltering accents whispered praise.
  At church, with meek and unaffected grace,
His looks adorned the venerable place;
Truth from his lips prevailed with double sway,
And fools, who came to scoff, remained to pray. 180
The service past, around the pious man,
With steady zeal, each honest rustic ran;
Even children followed with endearing wile,
And plucked his gown to share the good man's
    smile.
His ready smile a parent's warmth exprest; 185
Their welfare pleased him, and their cares distrest:
To them his heart, his love, his griefs were given,

But all his serious thoughts had rest in
    heaven.
As some tall cliff that lifts its awful form,
190 Swells from the vale, and midway leaves the
    storm,
Tho' round its breast the rolling clouds are
    spread,
Eternal sunshine settles on its head.
    Beside yon straggling fence that skirts the
    way,
With blossom'd furze unprofitably gay,
195 There, in his noisy mansion, skill'd to rule,
The village master taught his little school.
A man severe he was, and stern to view;
I knew him well, and every truant knew:
Well had the boding tremblers learned to
    trace
200 The day's disasters in his morning face;
Full well they laughed with counterfeited glee
At all his jokes, for many a joke had he;
Full well the busy whisper circling round
Conveyed the dismal tidings when he frowned.
205 Yet he was kind, or, if severe in aught,
The love he bore to learning was in fault;

The village all declared how much he knew:
'Twas certain he could write, and cypher too;
Lands he could measure, terms and tides presage,
And even the story ran that he could gauge: 210
In arguing, too, the parson owned his skill,
For, even tho' vanquished, he could argue still;
While words of learned length and thundering
    sound
Amazed the gazing rustics ranged around;
And still they gazed, and still the wonder grew, 215
That one small head could carry all he knew.
    But past is all his fame. The very spot
Where many a time he triumphed is forgot.
Near yonder thorn, that lifts its head on high,
Where once the sign-post caught the passing
    eye, 220
Low lies that house where nut-brown draughts
    inspired,
Where grey-beard mirth and smiling toil retired,
Where village statesmen talked with looks pro-
    found,
And news much older than their ale went round.
Imagination fondly stoops to trace 225
The parlor splendors of that festive place:

The white-washed wall, the nicely sanded
 floor,
The varnished clock that clicked behind the
 door;
The chest contrived a double debt to pay,
230 A bed by night, a chest of drawers by day;
The pictures placed for ornament and use,
The twelve good rules, the royal game of
 goose;
The hearth, except when winter chill'd the
 day,
With aspen boughs and flowers and fennel gay;
235 While broken tea-cups, wisely kept for shew,
Ranged o'er the chimney, glistened in a row.
 Vain transitory splendors! could not all
Reprieve the tottering mansion from its fall?
Obscure it sinks, nor shall it more impart
240 An hour's importance to the poor man's heart.
Thither no more the peasant shall repair
To sweet oblivion of his daily care;
No more the farmer's news, the barber's tale,
No more the wood-man's ballad shall prevail;
245 No more the smith his dusky brow shall clear,
Relax his ponderous strength, and lean to hear;

The host himself no longer shall be found
Careful to see the mantling bliss go round;
Nor the coy maid, half willing to be prest,
Shall kiss the cup to pass it to the rest.   250
   Yes! let the rich deride, the proud disdain,
These simple blessings of the lowly train;
To me more dear, congenial to my heart,
One native charm, than all the gloss of art;
Spontaneous joys, where Nature has its play,   255
The soul adopts, and owns their first born sway;
Lightly they frolic o'er the vacant mind,
Unenvied, unmolested, unconfined.
But the long pomp, the midnight masquerade,
With all the freaks of wanton wealth arrayed —   260
In these, ere triflers half their wish obtain,
The toiling pleasure sickens into pain;
And, e'en while fashion's brightest arts decoy,
The heart distrusting asks if this be joy.
   Ye friends to truth, ye statesmen who survey   265
The rich man's joys increase, the poor's decay,
Tis yours to judge, how wide the limits stand
Between a splendid and an happy land.
Proud swells the tide with loads of freighted ore,
And shouting Folly hails them from her shore;   270

Hoards e'en beyond the miser's wish abound,
And rich men flock from all the world around.
Yet count our gains.   This wealth is but a
    name
That leaves our useful products still the same.
275 Not so the loss.   The man of wealth and pride
Takes up a space that many poor supplied;
Space for his lake, his park's extended bounds,
Space for his horses, equipage, and hounds:
The robe that wraps his limbs in silken sloth
280 Has robbed the neighboring fields of half their
    growth;
His seat, where solitary sports are seen,
Indignant spurns the cottage from the green:
Around the world each needful product flies,
For all the luxuries the world supplies;
285 While thus the land adorned for pleasure all
In barren splendor feebly waits the fall.

    As some fair female unadorned and plain,
Secure to please while youth confirms her
    reign,
Slights every borrowed charm that dress
    supplies,
290 Nor shares with art the triumph of her eyes;

But when those charms are past, for charms are
    frail,
When time advances, and when lovers fail,
She then shines forth, solicitous to bless,
In all the glaring impotence of dress.
Thus fares the land by luxury betrayed: 295
In nature's simplest charms at first arrayed,
But verging to decline, its splendors rise;
Its vistas strike, its palaces surprise:
While, scourged by famine from the smiling land,
The mournful peasant leads his humble band, 300
And while he sinks, without one arm to save,
The country blooms — a garden and a grave.

    Where then, ah! where, shall poverty reside,
To scape the pressure of contiguous pride?
If to some common's fenceless limits strayed   305
He drives his flock to pick the scanty blade,
Those fenceless fields the sons of wealth divide,
And even the bare-worn common is denied.

    If to the city sped — what waits him there?
To see profusion that he must not share;   310
To see ten thousand baneful arts combined
To pamper luxury, and thin mankind;
To see those joys the sons of pleasure know

Extorted from his fellow-creature's woe.

315 Here while the courtier glitters in brocade,
There the pale artist plies the sickly trade;
Here while the proud their long-drawn pomps
    display,
There the black gibbet glooms beside the way.
The dome where pleasure holds her midnight
    reign

320 Here, richly deckt, admits the gorgeous train:
Tumultuous grandeur crowds the blazing
    square,
The rattling chariots clash, the torches glare.
Sure scenes like these no troubles e'er annoy!
Sure these denote one universal joy!

325 Are these thy serious thoughts? — Ah, turn
    thine eyes
Where the poor houseless shivering female lies.
She once, perhaps, in village plenty blest,
Has wept at tales of innocence distrest;
Her modest looks the cottage might adorn,

330 Sweet as the primrose peeps beneath the
    thorn:
Now lost to all; her friends, her virtue fled,
Near her betrayer's door she lays her head,

And, pinch'd with cold, and shrinking from the
    shower,
With heavy heart deplores that luckless hour,
When idly first, ambitious of the town,   335
She left her wheel and robes of country brown.
    Do thine, sweet Auburn, — thine, the loveliest
    train, —
Do thy fair tribes participate her pain?
Even now, perhaps, by cold and hunger led,
At proud men's doors they ask a little bread!   340
    Ah, no! To distant climes, a dreary scene,
Where half the convex world intrudes between,
Through torrid tracts with fainting steps they go,
Where wild Altama murmurs to their woe.
Far different there from all that charm'd before 345
The various terrors of that horrid shore;
Those blazing suns that dart a downward ray,
And fiercely shed intolerable day;
Those matted woods, where birds forget to sing,
But silent bats in drowsy clusters cling;   350
Those poisonous fields with rank luxuriance
    crowned,
Where the dark scorpion gathers death around;
Where at each step the stranger fears to wake

The rattling terrors of the vengeful snake;
355 Where crouching tigers wait their hapless prey,
And savage men more murderous still than
   they;
While oft in whirls the mad tornado flies,
Mingling the ravaged landscape with the skies.
Far different these from every former scene,
360 The cooling brook, the grassy vested green,
The breezy covert of the warbling grove,
That only sheltered thefts of harmless love.
   Good Heaven! what sorrows gloom'd that
      parting day,
That called them from their native walks
   away;
365 When the poor exiles, every pleasure past,
Hung .round the bowers, and fondly looked
   their last,
And took a long farewell, and wished in vain
For seats like these beyond the western main,
And shuddering still to face the distant deep,
370 Returned and wept, and still returned to weep.
The good old sire the first prepared to go
To new found worlds, and wept for others'
   woe;

But for himself, in conscious virtue brave,
He only wished for worlds beyond the grave.
His lovely daughter, lovelier in her tears,   375
The fond companion of his helpless years,
Silent went next, neglectful of her charms,
And left a lover's for a father's arms.
With louder plaints the mother spoke her woes,
And blest the cot where every pleasure rose,   380
And kist her thoughtless babes with many a tear,
And claspt them close, in sorrow doubly dear,
Whilst her fond husband strove to lend relief
In all the silent manliness of grief.

O luxury! thou curst by Heaven's decree,   385
How ill exchanged are things like these for thee!
How do thy potions, with insidious joy,
Diffuse their pleasure only to destroy!
Kingdoms by thee, to sickly greatness grown,
Boast of a florid vigor not their own.   390
At every draught more large and large they grow,
A bloated mass of rank unwieldy woe;
Till sapped their strength, and every part unsound,
Down, down they sink, and spread a ruin round.

Even now the devastation is begun,   395
And half the business of destruction done;

Even now, methinks, as pondering here I
    stand,
I see the rural virtues leave the land.
Down where yon anchoring vessel spreads the
    sail,
400 That idly waiting flaps with every gale,
Downward they move, a melancholy band,
Pass from the shore, and darken all the
    strand.
Contented toil, and hospitable care,
And kind connubial tenderness, are there;
405 And piety with wishes placed above,
And steady loyalty, and faithful love.
And thou, sweet Poetry, thou loveliest maid,
Still first to fly where sensual joys invade;
Unfit in these degenerate times of shame
410 To catch the heart, or strike for honest fame;
Dear charming nymph, neglected and decried,
My shame in crowds, my solitary pride;
Thou source of all my bliss, and all my woe,
That found'st me poor at first, and keep'st
    me so;
415 Thou guide by which the nobler arts excel,
Thou nurse of every virtue, fare thee well!

Farewell, and O! where'er thy voice be tried,
On Torno's cliffs, or Pambamarca's side,
Whether where equinoctial fervors glow,
Or winter wraps the polar world in snow,   420
Still let thy voice, prevailing over time,
Redress the rigors of the inclement clime;
Aid slighted truth with thy persuasive strain;
Teach erring man to spurn the rage of gain;
Teach him, that states of native strength possest,
Tho' very poor, may still be very blest;   426
That trade's proud empire hastes to swift decay,
As ocean sweeps the labored mole away;
While self-dependent power can time defy,
As rocks resist the billows and the sky.   430

THE HERMIT

"TURN, gentle Hermit of the dale,
    And guide my lonely way
To where yon taper cheers the vale
    With hospitable ray.

5   "For here forlorn and lost I tread,
    With fainting steps and slow,
Where wilds, immeasurably spread,
    Seem lengthening as I go."

"Forbear, my son," the Hermit cries,
10   "To tempt the dangerous gloom;
For yonder faithless phantom flies
    To lure thee to thy doom.

"Here to the houseless child of want
    My door is open still;
15 And though my portion is but scant,
    I give it with good will.

"Then turn to-night, and freely share
    Whate'er my cell bestows,
My rushy couch and frugal fare,
20   My blessing and repose.

"No flocks that range the valley free,
    To slaughter I condemn;
Taught by that Power that pities me,
    I learn to pity them:

"But from the mountain's grassy side,   25
    A guiltless feast I bring,
A scrip with herbs and fruits supplied,
    And water from the spring.

"Then, pilgrim, turn; thy cares forego;
    All earth-born cares are wrong: 30
Man wants but little here below,
    Nor wants that little long."

Soft as the dew from heaven descends,
    His gentle accents fell:
The modest stranger lowly bends,   35
    And follows to the cell.

Far in the wilderness obscure,
    The lonely mansion lay,
A refuge to the neighboring poor,
    And strangers led astray.   40

No stores beneath its humble thatch
Required a master's care;
The wicket, opening with a latch,
Received the harmless pair.

45 And now, when busy crowds retire
To take their evening rest,
The Hermit trimmed his little fire,
And cheered his pensive guest:

And spread his vegetable store,
50 And gaily pressed and smiled;
And skilled in legendary lore,
The lingering hours beguiled.

Around in sympathetic mirth,
Its tricks the kitten tries,
55 The cricket chirrups on the hearth,
The crackling fagot flies.

But nothing could a charm impart
To soothe the stranger's woe;
For grief was heavy at his heart,
60 And tears began to flow.

His rising cares the Hermit spied,
   With answering care opprest:
"And whence, unhappy youth," he cried,
   "The sorrows of thy breast?

"From better habitations spurned,   65
   Reluctant dost thou rove?
Or grieve for friendship unreturned,
   Or unregarded love?

"Alas! the joys that fortune brings,
   Are trifling, and decay;   70
And those who prize the paltry things
   More trifling still than they.

"And what is friendship but a name,
   A charm that lulls to sleep,
A shade that follows wealth or fame,   75
   But leaves the wretch to weep?

"And love is still an emptier sound,
   The modern fair one's jest;
On earth unseen, or only found
   To warm the turtle's nest.   80

"For shame, fond youth, thy sorrows hush,
    And spurn the sex," he said:
But, while he spoke, a rising blush
    His love-lorn guest betrayed.

85 Surprised, he sees new beauties rise,
    Swift mantling to the view;
Like colors o'er the morning skies,
    As bright, as transient too.

The bashful look, the rising breast,
90   Alternate spread alarms:
The lovely stranger stands confest,
    A maid in all her charms.

"And, ah! forgive a stranger rude,
    A wretch forlorn," she cried;
95 "Whose feet unhallowed thus intrude
    Where heaven and you reside.

"But let a maid thy pity share,
    Whom love has taught to stray;
Who seeks for rest, but finds despair
100   Companion of her way.

"My father lived beside the Tyne;
  A wealthy lord was he;
And all his wealth was mark'd as mine, —
  He had but only me.

"To win me from his tender arms,   105
  Unnumbered suitors came,
Who praised me for imputed charms,
  And felt or feigned a flame.

"Each hour a mercenary crowd
  With richest proffers strove;   110
Amongst the rest young Edwin bowed,
  But never talked of love.

"In humble, simplest habits clad,
  No wealth nor power had he;
Wisdom and worth were all he had,   115
  But these were all to me.

"And when beside me in the dale,
  He carolled lays of love,
His breath lent fragrance to the gale,
  And music to the grove.   120

"The blossom opening to the day,
  The dews of heaven refined,
Could nought of purity display,
  To emulate his mind.

125 "The dew, the blossom on the tree,
       With charms inconstant shine;
     Their charms were his, but, woe to me!
       Their constancy was mine.

     "For still I tried each fickle art,
130   Importunate and vain;
     And while his passion touched my heart,
       I triumphed in his pain.

     "Till, quite dejected with my scorn,
       He left me to my pride,
135 And sought a solitude forlorn,
       In secret, where he died.

     "But mine the sorrow, mine the fault,
       And well my life shall pay;
     I'll seek the solitude he sought,
140   And stretch me where he lay.

"And there forlorn, despairing, hid,
    I'll lay me down and die;
'Twas so for me that Edwin did,
    And so for him will I."

"Forbid it, Heaven!" the Hermit cried,   145
    And clasped her to his breast:
The wondering fair one turn'd to chide, —
    'Twas Edwin's self that pressed!

"Turn, Angelina, ever dear;
    My charmer, turn to see   150
Thy own, thy long-lost Edwin here,
    Restored to love and thee.

"Thus let me hold thee to my heart,
    And every care resign:
And shall we never, never part,   155
    My life — my all that's mine?

"No, never from this hour to part
    We'll live and love so true,
The sigh that rends thy constant heart
    Shall break thy Edwin's too."   160

A DESCRIPTION OF AN AUTHOR'S BEDCHAMBER

WHERE the Red Lion, staring o'er the way,
Invites each passing stranger that can pay;
Where Calvert's butt, and Parson's black
    champagne,
Regale the drabs and bloods of Drury-lane;
5 There, in a lonely room, from bailiffs snug,
The muse found Scroggen stretch'd beneath a
    rug;
A window, patch'd with paper, lent a ray,
That dimly show'd the state in which he lay;
The sanded floor that grits beneath the tread;
10 The humid wall with paltry pictures spread;
The royal game of goose was there in view,
And the twelve rules the royal martyr drew;
The seasons, fram'd with listing, found a place,
And brave prince William show'd his lamp-
    black face.
15 The morn was cold; he views with keen desire
The rusty grate unconscious of a fire:
With beer and milk arrears the frieze was
    scor'd,

And five crack'd teacups dress'd the chimney
    board;
A nightcap deck'd his brows instead of bay,
A cap by night, — a stocking all the day!   20

AN ELEGY ON THE DEATH OF A
MAD DOG

GOOD people all, of every sort,
    Give ear unto my song;
And if you find it wondrous short, —
    It cannot hold you long.

In Islington there was a man,   5
    Of whom the world might say,
That still a godly race he ran, —
    Whene'er he went to pray.

A kind and gentle heart he had,
    To comfort friends and foes;   10
The naked every day he clad, —
    When he put on his clothes.

And in that town a dog was found,
    As many dogs there be,

15 Both mongrel, puppy, whelp, and hound,
   And curs of low degree.

   This dog and man at first were friends;
     But when a pique began,
   The dog, to gain some private ends,
20   Went mad, and bit the man.

   Around from all the neighboring streets
     The wondering neighbors ran,
   And swore the dog had lost his wits,
     To bite so good a man.

25 The wound it seem'd both sore and sad
     To every Christian eye;
   And while they swore the dog was mad,
     They swore the man would die.

   But soon a wonder came to light,
30   That show'd the rogues they lied:
   The man recover'd of the bite,
     The dog it was that died.

AN ELEGY ON THAT GLORY OF HER SEX, MRS. MARY BLAIZE

Good people all, with one accord,
    Lament for Madam Blaize,
Who never wanted a good word —
    From those who spoke her praise.

The needy seldom pass'd her door,   5
    And always found her kind;
She freely lent to all the poor —
    Who left a pledge behind.

She strove the neighborhood to please
    With manners wondrous winning;   10
And never follow'd wicked ways —
    Unless when she was sinning.

At church, in silks and satins new,
    With hoop of monstrous size,
She never slumber'd in her pew —   15
    But when she shut her eyes.

Her love was sought, I do aver,
    By twenty beaux and more;

The king himself has follow'd her —
20 When she has walk'd before.

But now, her wealth and finery fled,
  Her hangers-on cut short all;
The doctors found, when she was dead —
  Her last disorder mortal.

25 Let us lament in sorrow sore,
  For Kent Street well may say,
That had she lived a twelvemonth more —
  She had not died to-day.

WHEN LOVELY WOMAN STOOPS TO FOLLY

WHEN lovely woman stoops to folly,
  And finds too late that men betray,
What charm can soothe her melancholy?
  What art can wash her guilt away?

5 The only art her guilt to cover,
  To hide her shame from every eye,
To give repentance to her lover,
  And wring his bosom, is — to die.

THE WRETCH CONDEMNED WITH LIFE TO PART

THE wretch condemned with life to part,
　　Still, still on hope relies;
And every pang, that rends the heart,
　　Bids expectation rise.

Hope, like the glimmering taper's light, 　5
　　Adorns and cheers the way;
And still, as darker grows the night,
　　Emits a brighter ray.

O MEMORY! THOU FOND DECEIVER

O MEMORY! thou fond deceiver,
　　Still importunate and vain,
To former joys recurring ever,
　　And turning all the past to pain.

Thou, like the world, the opprest oppressing, 5
　　Thy smiles increase the wretch's woe;
And he who wants each other blessing,
　　In thee must ever find a foe.

STANZAS ON THE TAKING OF QUEBEC

AMIDST the clamor of exulting joys,
  Which triumph forces from the patriot heart,
Grief dares to mingle her soul-piercing voice,
  And quells the raptures which from pleas-
    ure start.

5   O Wolfe! to thee a streaming flood of woe,
      Sighing, we pay, and think e'en conquest
        dear;
    Quebec in vain shall teach our breast to glow,
      Whilst thy sad fate extorts the heart-wrung
        tear.

    Alive, the foe thy dreadful vigor fled,
10   And saw thee fall with joy-pronouncing eyes:
    Yet they shall know thou conquerest, though
        dead!
      Since from thy tomb a thousand heroes rise.

THE HAUNCH OF VENISON

A POETICAL EPISTLE TO LORD CLARE

THANKS, my lord, for your venison, for finer or
    fatter
Ne'er ranged in a forest, or smoked in a platter.
The haunch was a picture for painters to study,
The fat was so white, and the lean was so ruddy;
Though my stomach was sharp, I could scarce
    help regretting   5
To spoil such a delicate picture by eating;
I had thoughts in my chambers to place it in
    view,
To be shown to my friends as a piece of *virtù;*
As in some Irish houses, where things are so so,
One gammon of bacon hangs up for a show: 10
But, for eating a rasher of what they take pride in,
They'd as soon think of eating the pan it is fried in.
But hold — let me pause — don't I hear you pro-
    nounce,
This tale of the bacon a damnable bounce?
Well, suppose it a bounce, — sure a poet may
    try,   15
By a bounce now and then, to get courage to fly.

But, my lord, it's no bounce: I protest, in
   my turn,
It's a truth — and your lordship may ask Mr.
   Bryne.
To go on with my tale: as I gazed on the
   haunch,
20 I thought of a friend that was trusty and
    staunch;
So I cut it, and sent it to Reynolds undrest,
To paint it, or eat it, just as he liked best.
Of the neck and the breast I had next to dis-
   pose —
'Twas a neck and a breast that might rival
   Monroe's:
25 But in parting with these I was puzzled again,
With the how, and the who, and the where,
   and the when.
There's Howard, and Coley, and H—rth, and
   Hiff,
I think they love venison — I know they love
   beef.
There's my countryman, Higgins — oh! let
   him alone,
30 For making a blunder, or picking a bone.

But, hang it! — to poets who seldom can eat,
Your very good mutton's a very good treat;
Such dainties to them their health it might hurt,
It's like sending them ruffles, when wanting a shirt.
While thus I debated, in reverie centered,   35
An acquaintance, a friend as he called himself,
     entered;
An under-bred, fine-spoken fellow was he,
And he smiled as he looked at the venison and me.
"What have we got here? — Why this is good
     eating!
Your own, I suppose — or is it in waiting?"   40
"Why, whose should it be?" cried I with a flounce,
"I get these things often" — but that was a
     bounce:
"Some lords, my acquaintance, that settle the
     nation,
Are pleased to be kind — but I hate ostentation."
     "If that be the case then," cried he, very gay,   45
"I'm glad I have taken this house in my way.
To-morrow you take a poor dinner with me;
No words — I insist on't — precisely at three;
We'll have Johnson, and Burke; all the wits will
     be there; ˙

50 My acquaintance is slight, or I'd ask my
    Lord Clare.
   And now that I think on't, as I am a sinner,
   We wanted this venison to make out the
    dinner.
   What say you — a pasty? It shall, and it
    must,
   And my wife, little Kitty, is famous for crust.
55 Here, porter! this venison with me to Mile-end:
   No stirring — I beg — my dear friend — my
    dear friend!"
   Thus, snatching his hat, he brushed off like
    the wind,
   And the porter and eatables followed behind.
    Left alone to reflect, having emptied my
    shelf,
60 And "nobody with me at sea but myself";
   Though I could not help thinking my gentle-
    man hasty,
   Yet Johnson, and Burke, and a good venison
    pasty,
   Were things that I never disliked in my life,
   Though clogg'd with a coxcomb, and Kitty
    his wife.

So next day, in due splendor to make my approach,   65
I drove to his door in my own hackney-coach.
   When come to the place where we all were to dine,
(A chair-lumbered closet just twelve feet by nine),
My friend bade me welcome, but struck me quite dumb
With tidings that Johnson and Burke would not come: 70
"For I knew it," he cried: "both eternally fail;
The one with his speeches, and t'other with Thrale.
But no matter, I'll warrant we'll make up the party
With two full as clever, and ten times as hearty.
The one is a Scotchman, the other a Jew;   75
They're both of them merry, and authors like you;
The one writes the Snarler, the other the Scourge;
Some thinks he writes Cinna — he owns to Panurge."
While thus he described them, by trade and by name,
They entered, and dinner was served as they came.   80

At the top a fried liver and bacon were seen;
At the bottom was tripe in a swinging tureen;
At the sides there was spinach and pudding
    made hot;
In the middle a place where the pasty — was
    not.
85 Now, my lord, as for tripe, it's my utter
    aversion,
And your bacon I hate like a Turk or a
    Persian;
So there I sat stuck like a horse in a pound,
While the bacon and liver went merrily
    round:
But what vex'd me most was that d——d
    Scottish rogue,
90 With his long-winded speeches, his smiles, and
    his brogue,
And, "Madam," quoth he, "may this bit be
    my poison,
A prettier dinner I never set eyes on;
Pray a slice of your liver, though may I be
    curst,
But I've eat of your tripe till I'm ready to
    burst."

"The tripe!" quoth the Jew, with his chocolate
    cheek,   95
"I could dine on this tripe seven days in a week:
I like these here dinners so pretty and small;
But your friend there, the doctor, eats nothing at
    all."
"O! ho!" quoth my friend, "he'll come on in a
    trice;
He's keeping a corner for something that's nice: 100
There's a pasty." — "A pasty!" repeated the Jew;
"I don't care if I keep a corner for't too."
"What, the deil, mon, a pasty!" re-echoed the
    Scot;
"Though splitting, I'll still keep a corner for that."
"We'll all keep a corner," the lady cried out; 105
"We'll all keep a corner," was echoed about.
While thus we resolved, and the pasty delayed,
With looks that quite petrified, entered the maid:
A visage so sad, and so pale with affright,
Waked Priam in drawing his curtains by night. 110
But we quickly found out — for who could mis-
    take her? —
That she came with some terrible news from the
    baker:

And so it fell out; for that negligent sloven
Had shut out the pasty on shutting his oven.
115 Sad Philomel thus — but let similes drop —
And now that I think on't, the story may
stop.
To be plain, my good lord, it's but labor
misplaced,
To send such good verses to one of your taste;
You've got an odd something — a kind of
discerning,
120 A relish, a taste — sickened over by learning;
At least it's your temper, as very well known,
That you think very slightly of all that's your
own:
So perhaps, in your habits of thinking amiss,
You may make a mistake, and think slightly
of this.

RETALIATION

OF old, when Scarron his companions invited,
Each guest brought his dish, and the feast
was united;
If our landlord supplies us with beef and with
fish,

Let each guest bring himself, and he brings the
  best dish:
Our Dean shall be venison, just fresh from the
  plains;   5
Our Burke shall be tongue, with a garnish of
  brains;
Our Will shall be wild-fowl, of excellent flavor,
And Dick with his pepper shall heighten the
  savor;
Our Cumberland's sweetbread its place shall ob-
  tain,
And Douglas is pudding, substantial and plain; 10
Our Garrick's a salad, for in him we see
Oil, vinegar, sugar, and saltness agree;
To make out the dinner, full certain I am,
That Ridge is anchovy, and Reynolds is lamb;
That Hickey's a capon, and, by the same rule, 15
Magnanimous Goldsmith a gooseberry fool.
At a dinner so various, at such a repast,
Who'd not be a glutton, and stick to the last?
Here, waiter, more wine! let me sit while I'm able,
Till all my companions sink under the table;   20
Then, with chaos and blunders encircling my head,
Let me ponder, and tell what I think of the dead.

Here lies the good Dean, re-united to earth,
Who mix'd reason with pleasure, and wisdom
   with mirth:
25 If he had any faults, he has left us in doubt —
At least, in six weeks, I could not find 'em
   out;
Yet some have declar'd, and it can't be denied
   'em,
That sly-boots was cursedly cunning to hide
   'em.

Here lies our good Edmund, whose genius
   was such,
30 We scarcely can praise it or blame it too
   much;
Who, born for the universe, narrow'd his mind,
And to party gave up what was meant for
   mankind;
Though fraught with all learning, yet straining
   his throat,
To persuade Tommy Townshend to lend him
   a vote;
35 Who, too deep for his hearers, still went on
   refining,

And thought of convincing, while they thought of
    dining;
Though equal to all things, for all things unfit;
Too nice for a statesman, too proud for a wit,
For a patriot too cool, for a drudge disobedient,
And too fond of the *right* to pursue the *expedient*.
In short, 'twas his fate, unemploy'd, or in place,
    sir,   41
To eat mutton cold, and cut blocks with a razor.

  Here lies honest William, whose heart was a
    mint,
While the owner ne'er knew half the good that was
    in't:
The pupil of impulse, it forc'd him along,   45
His conduct still right, with his argument wrong;
Still aiming at honor, yet fearing to roam,
The coachman was tipsy, the chariot drove home.
Would you ask for his merits? alas! he had none;
What was good was spontaneous, his faults were
    his own.   50

  Here lies honest Richard, whose fate I must
    sigh at;

Alas, that such frolic should now be so quiet!
What spirits were his! what wit and what
    whim!
Now breaking a jest, and now breaking a limb;
55 Now wrangling and grumbling to keep up the
    ball;
Now teasing and vexing, yet laughing at all!
In short, so provoking a devil was Dick,
That we wished him full ten times a-day at
    Old Nick;
But, missing his mirth and agreeable vein,
60 As often we wish'd to have Dick back again.

Here Cumberland lies, having acted his
    parts,
The Terence of England, the mender of hearts;
A flattering painter, who made it his care
To draw men as they ought to be, not as they
    are.
65 His gallants are all faultless, his women divine,
And comedy wonders at being so fine;
Like a tragedy queen he has dizen'd her out,
Or rather like tragedy giving a rout.
His fools have their follies so lost in a crowd

Of virtues and feelings, that folly grows proud; 70
And coxcombs, alike in their failings alone,
Adopting his portraits, are pleased with their
    own.
Say, where has our poet this malady caught?
Or wherefore his characters thus without fault?
Say, was it that vainly directing his view   75
To find out men's virtues, and finding them few,
Quite sick of pursuing each troublesome elf,
He grew lazy at last, and drew from himself?

    Here Douglas retires from his toils to relax,
The scourge of impostors, the terror of quacks: 80
Come, all ye quack bards, and ye quacking divines,
Come, and dance on the spot where your tyrant
    reclines!
When satire and censure encircled his throne,
I fear'd for your safety, I fear'd for my own;
But now he is gone, and we want a detector,   85
Our Dodds shall be pious, our Kenricks shall lec-
    ture,
Macpherson write bombast, and call it a style,
Our Townshend make speeches, and I shall com-
    pile;

New Lauders and Bowers the Tweed shall cross
    over,
90 No countryman living their tricks to discover;
Detection her taper shall quench to a spark,
And Scotchman meet Scotchman, and cheat
    in the dark.

Here lies David Garrick, describe him who
    can,
An abridgment of all that was pleasant in man;
95 As an actor, confess'd without rival to shine;
As a wit, if not first, in the very first line:
Yet, with talents like these, and an excellent
    heart,
The man had his failings, a dupe to his art.
Like an ill-judging beauty, his colors he spread,
100 And beplaster'd with rouge his own natural
    red.
On the stage he was natural, simple, affecting;
'Twas only that when he was off he was acting.
With no reason on earth to go out of his way,
He turn'd and he varied full ten times a day:
105 Though secure of our hearts, yet confoundedly
    sick.

If they were not his own by finessing and trick:
He cast off his friends, as a huntsman his pack,
For he knew when he pleased he could whistle
    them back.
Of praise a mere glutton, he swallow'd what came,
And the puff of a dunce he mistook it for fame; 110
Till his relish grown callous, almost to disease,
Who pepper'd the highest was surest to please.
But let us be candid, and speak out our mind,
If dunces applauded, he paid them in kind.
Ye Kenricks, ye Kellys, and Woodfalls so grave, 115
What a commerce was yours, while you got and
    you gave!
How did Grub-street re-echo the shouts that you
    raised,
While he was be-Roscius'd, and you were be-
    praised!
But peace to his spirit, wherever it flies,
To act as an angel and mix with the skies: 120
Those poets who owe their best fame to his skill,
Shall still be his flatterers, go where he will;
Old Shakspeare receive him with praise and with
    love,
And Beaumonts and Bens be his Kellys above.

125   Here Hickey reclines, a most blunt, pleasant creature,
And slander itself must allow him good nature;
He cherish'd his friend, and he relish'd a bumper;
Yet one fault he had, and that one was a thumper.
Perhaps you may ask if the man was a miser?
130   I answer, no, no; for he always was wiser.
Too courteous, perhaps, or obligingly flat?
His very worst foe can't accuse him of that.
Perhaps he confided in men as they go,
And so was too foolishly honest? Ah, no!
135   Then what was his failing? come tell it, and burn ye!
He was — could he help it? — a special attorney.

Here Reynolds is laid, and, to tell you my mind,
He has not left a wiser or better behind:
His pencil was striking, resistless, and grand,
140   His manners were gentle, complying, and bland:

Still born to improve us in every part,
His pencil our faces, his manners our heart.
To coxcombs averse, yet most civilly steering,
When they judged without skill, he was still hard
    of hearing;
When they talked of their Raphaels, Correggios,
    and stuff,   145
He shifted his trumpet, and only took snuff.

POSTSCRIPT

Here Whitefoord reclines, and deny it who can,
Though he merrily liv'd, he is now a grave man:
Rare compound of oddity, frolic, and fun!
Who relish'd a joke, and rejoic'd in a pun;
Whose temper was generous, open, sincere;
A stranger to flattery, a stranger to fear;
Who scatter'd around wit and humor at will;
Whose daily *bon mots* half a column might fill:
A Scotchman, from pride and from prejudice free;
A scholar, yet surely no pedant was he.

What pity, alas! that so liberal a mind
Should so long be to newspaper essays confin'd!
Who perhaps to the summit of science could soar,
Yet content "if the table he set in a roar";
Whose talents to fill any station was fit,
Yet happy if Woodfall confess'd him a wit.

Ye newspaper witlings! ye pert scribbling folks!
Who copied his squibs, and re-echoed his jokes;

Ye tame imitators, ye servile herd, come
Still follow your master, and visit his tomb:
To deck it, bring with you festoons of the vine
And copious libations bestow on his shrine;
Then strew all around it (you can do no less)
Cross readings, ship news, and mistakes of the press.

Merry Whitefoord, farewell! for thy sake I admit
That a Scot may have humor, I had almost said wit:
This debt to thy memory I cannot refuse,
"Thou best-humored man with the worst humor'd muse."

NOTES

NOTES ON *THE TRAVELER*

THE first draft of *The Traveler* was some lines which Goldsmith wrote in 1755, when in Switzerland, and enclosed in a letter to his brother Henry. We do not know which lines these were, but they were probably the introductory ones about his home and his brother, and possibly the ones describing Switzerland. Some years later, this fragment, with some changes and additions, was shown to Dr. Johnson, who commended it and urged Goldsmith to complete the poem. Dr. Johnson suggested for it the title of *The Philosophic Wanderer*, which Goldsmith had the good taste to reject, though he accepted some of his friend's rather stately lines. You will find, on page seventeen of the Introduction, an account of the writing and publication of *The Traveler*. It came out in a quarto volume, December 19, 1764, dated 1765, and was the first of Goldsmith's works which bore his name on the title page. Like all his other poems, it was written slowly and polished with scrupulous care. The early editions of *The Traveler*, which he corrected, are full of improvements, — changed words, couplets, whole passages.

The poem is written in the 'heroic couplet,' favored by Dryden, Pope, Johnson, and other poets of the classical schools. By examining the poem, you will see that each line consists of ten syllables, an unaccented one being regularly followed by an accented one; the lines rhyme in couplets. This meter is adapted to a formal, rather precise style. Goldsmith, who marks the transition between classicism and romanticism in English poetry, gave the classic meter a natural beauty, a grace and charm which it had never had before.

According to the customs of the time, the poem has a didactic theme, — the opinion that political institutions do not affect man's happiness, which depends on himself alone, and that one form of government is as good as another. We, of course, do not agree with this opinion, which was held by Goldsmith and his friend Dr. Johnson. Boswell, ever jealous for the fame of his idol, suggested that *The Traveler* owed its charm to the thoughts gleaned by Goldsmith, 'as a kind of poetical reporter,' from the conversation of Dr. Johnson. Goldsmith probably got a few suggestions from various sources, — some from Dr. Johnson's *Vanity of Human Wishes*, some from Addison's *Letter from Italy*, some from Thompson's long, dull poem on *Liberty* — but the poem as a whole is his very own, original and inimitable.

Title: 'Prospect' is here used in the sense of 'view.' 'Society' means the social and political condition of mankind. Is this the meaning we usually attach to the word 'society'?

1. "The very first line of the poem strikes a keynote; there is in it a pathetic thrill of distance and regret and longing; and it has the soft musical sound that pervades the whole composition." — *Black*.

Slow: "Chamier once asked him what he meant by 'slow,' the last word in the first line of *The Traveler*:

'Remote, unfriended, melancholy, slow.'

'Did he mean tardiness of locomotion?' Goldsmith, who would say something without consideration, answered 'Yes.' I was sitting by and said, 'No, sir; you do not mean tardiness of locomotion; you mean that sluggishness of mind which comes upon a man in solitude.' Chamier believed then that I had written the line as much as if he had seen me write it." — *Johnson in Boswell's Life of Johnson.* The essential thing is that the poet used the right word, appropriate in its twofold meaning.

2. **Or . . . or:** Either . . . or.

Scheld, Po: Where are these rivers? Why is the word 'lazy,' in the sense of slow-moving, applicable to the rivers of Belgium and Holland? Could this adjective be applied to the Po?

3. **Carinthian boor:** Carinthia is a province of Austria. Goldsmith visited it in his wanderings in 1755, and was denied a night's lodging by a churlish peasant.

5. **Campania:** Probably there is meant, instead of the Italian province, the Campagna of Rome, a desolate, deserted plain.

10. Goldsmith expresses this same sentiment in *The Citizen of the World:* "The farther I travel, I feel the pain of separation with stronger force; those ties that bind me to my native country and you are still unbroken; by every remove I only drag a greater length of chain." The chain of memory, he suggests, holds him to his brother, as the chain fastened to the ankles of criminals confines them.

13–22. Compare *The Deserted Village*, lines 149–162.

15. **Want and pain:** Those who suffer want and pain.

24. In his young manhood, Goldsmith spent several years wandering about Europe. He traveled on foot through Germany, France, Switzerland, and Italy. In the twentieth chapter of *The Vicar of Wakefield*, he gives, in the person of George Primrose, an account of his journeyings.

25–28. These lines, it will be observed, are parenthetical.

27–28. The beautiful description of the horizon that seems to retreat from us. Compare the lines in Tennyson's *Ulysses:*

"Yet all experience is an arch where through
Shines that untraveled world whose margin falls
Forever and forever as we move."

29. **Leads:** This verb has for its object 'me,' in line 23.

31–36. In imagination, Goldsmith places himself in a position most appropriate to the train of thought which he is about to indulge, — upon a lofty peak of the Alps, below which the countries of Europe are spread like a map.

34. **An hundred:** An was the original form of the adjective, now 'a' and 'an.' In Goldsmith's time 'an' was still used before words beginning with a consonant or a sounded *h*, where we would now use 'a.'

42. **School-taught pride:** Pride taught in the schools, as of the Stoic philosophers, who claimed that good fortune or ill was a matter of indifference to them.

48. **Swains:** Young countrymen; its original meaning is 'servants.' It was a favorite word with the poets of the eighteenth century, and was used somewhat vaguely to designate lovers, shepherds, or any young country men.

Dress: Till. See Genesis ii, 15.

49–50. In what sense is this true?

57–62. No one ever gave sympathy or money more freely to relieve the wants of others than did Goldsmith. From the college days when he gave the coat from his back and the blankets from his bed to a poor widow, he was ever ready to share his last penny or rag or crust with those in need.

57. **Sorrows fall:** That is, tears, the signs of sorrow.

69. **Line:** The equator, the imaginary line dividing the earth.

70. **Palmy:** Made from the sap of the palm.

77. What is the force of 'shall' here? What difference would 'will' make in the meaning of the sentence?

Wisdom: That is, the man possessing wisdom.

81. Compare Byron's *Childe Harold:*

"Dear Nature is the kindest mother still."

84. **Idra:** Idria, a mountain town on the rocky banks of the river Idria in Austria.

Arno: Where is this river, and what famous cities are on its banks?

Shelvy side: Gently sloping banks.

87–98. Goldsmith here expresses the view, which later formed the main theme of *The Deserted Village.* He expresses the same opinion in prose. Do you think it is correct?

90. **Either:** Each.

91–92. These lines are explanatory of line 90.

92. Compare the line in Tennyson's *Locksley Hall:*

"And the jingling of the guinea helps the hurt that honor feels."

98. **Peculiar pain:** Pain peculiar to itself.

100. **The prospect:** That is, the view from the Alpine height.

101. **My proper cares:** Cares peculiar to me.

106. **Between:** What words are here to be supplied in thought?

115. **Blooms:** Blossoms.

119. **Kindred:** Kin, or like in kind, to that native to them.

121. **Gelid:** Congealed; cold; — here, 'pleasingly cool' (?)

122. **Winnow:** Waft, diffuse, without the idea of separating which this verb usually has.

124. **Sensual bliss:** That is, the bliss derived from the senses, without the idea of vice.

The nation: That is, the Italian nation.

130. Even while he confesses and does penance for one sin, he plans another.

133. At the close of the Middle Ages, the Italian cities — especially Florence, Genoa, Pisa, and Venice — controlled the commerce of Europe.

135–136. Compare the lines in Addison's *Letter from Italy:*

"Here domes and temples rise in distant views,
And opening palaces invite my muse."

136. **Long-fallen:** That is, since the days of Roman power.

137–138. Compare Addison's *Letter from Italy:*

"The smooth chisel all its force has shown
And softened into flesh the rugged stone . . .
So warm with life his [Raphael's] colors glow."

Name some of the famous architects, sculptors, and painters who were the glory of Italy and the world about the close of the Middle Ages.

139–140. The discovery of America and of the sea-route to India were the two chief causes of the decay of Italian commerce.

142. **Unmanned:** Depopulated.

143. **Skill:** Knowledge, its old meaning.

144. Goldsmith expresses this same thought in *The Citizen of the World:* "The state resembled one of those bodies bloated with disease, whose bulk is only a symptom of its wretchedness. Their former opulence only rendered them more impotent."

145–164. Italy was often and justly reproached for its servile condition, so unworthy of the power and wealth and genius of the past. About the middle of the nineteenth century, there arose a band of patriots that secured its freedom and national unity.

150–151. The Italians are especially fond of parades and processions.

152. **Mistress:** Lady-love.

153–154. On page seventeen in the Introduction is an incident about the composition of these lines.

159. **Domes:** Stately buildings, the old meaning of the word. It is now restricted in meaning to the cupola above a building.

Caesars: Who were they?

163. **Pile:** Building.

165–174. Does Goldsmith seem to admire Swiss scenery? Notice the phrases that he uses: "bleak," "barren hills," "torpid rocks," "stormy glooms." Picturesque beauty and rugged grandeur did not appeal to the classic poets whose ideals of beauty were derived from the Greek. "Every Homeric landscape intended to be beautiful," says Ruskin, "is composed of a fountain, a meadow, and a shady grove."

167. **Bleak Swiss:** Why does the poet call the people 'bleak'?

170. From the fifteenth century through the French Revolution, the Swiss were the chief mercenary soldiers of Europe.

171. **Vernal:** This was a favorite word with eighteenth-century poets.

176. **Redress:** Compensate for.

181-182. These lines depend on the verb 'sees' in line 179.

181. Explain the word 'costly,' as applied to 'lord.'

182. In many parts of Europe, especially in France, the use of meat was almost unknown among the poorer classes, in Goldsmith's day. It was estimated that the consumption of meat among French peasants in 1760 did not amount to more than a pound a month for each person.

187. **Finny deep:** Explain this expression. In *The Citizen of the World* Goldsmith speaks of fish as "finny prey."

190. **Savage:** Wild beast. In what sense do we use 'savage' as a noun?

191. **Sped:** Performed. As in the expression, 'God speed you,' the word here conveys the idea of prosperity, not haste.

197-198. It was thus that Goldsmith, during his wanderings in Europe, often paid for his lodgings.

198. **Nightly:** For the night.

216. **Supplies:** Satisfies.

217. See note on line 124.

221. **Level:** Unvaried; monotonous.

224. **Of:** This word connects 'once a year' with 'festival,' which it modifies.

228. **Morals:** Manners, — the Latin *mores*.

234. **Cowering:** Brooding, not crouching as with fear.

243-254. Goldsmith here speaks of his wandering days, more fully described, in the person of George Primrose, in the twentieth chapter of *The Vicar of Wakefield*. The poet's friends inform us that he could not read music, but played the flute fairly well by ear.

244. **Loire:** Where is this river?

253. **Gestic:** Gesticulating. Dancing is sometimes termed the 'gestic art.'

265–266. Observe how much thought is packed here in a few words.

273. **Tawdry:** Gaudy; showy. Tawdry was originally applied to any toy or finery bought at a fair held on St. Awdry's day, and because these were usually gaudy trinkets, the word came to have its present meaning.

276. **Frieze:** A coarse woolen cloth.

277. **Cheer:** Food. Is this a common meaning of the word?

286. **Rampire:** Rampart, — that is, dike.

290. As you doubtless know, much of the territory of Holland has been rescued by dikes and canals from the ocean. Works are now on hand which will enlarge the country an eighth. Goldsmith, in his *Animated Nature*, says: "The whole kingdom of Holland seems to be a conquest on the sea, and in a manner rescued from its bosom. The surface of the earth in this country is below the level of the bed of the sea; and I remember upon approaching the coast to have looked down upon it from the sea as into a valley."

303. **Are:** The subject is 'good'; why is the verb plural in form?

305–312. Is Goldsmith just to the Dutch in this description of their character?

309. Goldsmith uses the same words in *The Citizen of the World:* "A nation once famous for setting the world an example of freedom is now become a land of tyrants and a den of slaves."

311. **Bent:** That is, to the yoke of bondage.

313. Goldsmith confuses the Dutch and the Belgians.

317. **Genius:** Poetic muse.

318–323. Goldsmith says of Britain in *The Citizen of the World:* "Yet from the vernal softness of the air, the verdure of the fields, the transparency of the streams and the beauty of the women; here love might sport among painted lawns and warbling groves, and carol upon gales wafting at once both fragrance and harmony." Such were the beauties which appealed to Goldsmith and the other classic poets who preceded Wordsworth and the romantic poets.

319. Arcadia in Greece was the favorite scene of pastoral romances. Sir Philip Sidney and other poets and romancers described it as an ideal land of beauty and happiness.

320. **Hydaspes:** The modern Jelum, a river of India.

332. **Imagined right:** That which he imagines is his right.

333. Boasts that he scans these rights, — that is, that he considers them and has a voice in the government.

345. **Ferments:** Political disturbances.

Imprisoned: That is, by the bounds of law.

357. **Stems:** Families.

358. **Wrote:** In Goldsmith's time, this was the common participal form of the verb 'write.' What do we use now?

362. In the poet's words when the Duke of Northumberland would have patronized him, we have a proof of his manly independence. See page eighteen of the Introduction.

363–380. In place of these lines, there was in the first edition only these two lines:

"Perish the wish, for inly satisfied,
Above their pomps, I hold my ragged pride."

Forster thought that Goldsmith omitted the "ragged pride," 'because it involved an undignified admission,' but we prefer to believe him animated by desire to improve the poem.

382. Goldsmith says in the preface to his *History of England:* "It is not yet decided in politics whether the diminution of kingly power in England tends to increase the happiness or the freedom of the people. For my own part, from seeing the bad effects of the tyranny of the great in those republican states that pretend to be free, I cannot help wishing that our monarchs may still be allowed to enjoy the power of controlling the encroachments of the great at home."

386. Goldsmith expresses the same thought in the nine-

teenth chapter of *The Vicar of Wakefield:* "What they may then expect, may be seen by turning our eyes to Holland, Genoa, or Venice, where the laws govern the poor and the rich govern the law."

396. Gave wealth: That is, gave to wealth. 'Wealth' is the indirect object of the verb; what is the direct object?

397–412. This is the main didactic theme of *The Deserted Village.*

410–422. See *The Deserted Village,* lines 341–362.

411. Where is the Oswego River?

412. The accent of 'Niagara' was formerly on the next to the last syllable, as here.

416. When his poem was written, the horrors of the French and Indian wars were still fresh in the minds of Englishmen.

420. Dr. Johnson wrote this line. A critic, Leslie Stephen, says: "When Johnson prunes or interpolates lines in *The Traveler,* we feel as though a woodsman's ax was hacking at a most delicate piece of carving."

427. "Every mind," says Goldsmith in *The Citizen of the World,* "seems capable of entertaining a certain quantity of happiness, which no constitutions can increase, no circumstances alter, and entirely independent of fortune."

429–434. These lines were written by Dr. Johnson.

436. Luke's iron crown: Two brothers, George and Luke Dosa, led a revolt of Hungarian peasants in 1514; George, not Luke, was tortured by having a red-hot iron crown put upon his head, as punishment for allowing the peasants to proclaim him king of Hungary.

Damiens' bed of steel: Robert François Damiens, who endeavored, in 1757, to assassinate King Louis XV. of France, was put in an iron chair and tortured, then put to death.

437–438. These lines were written by Dr. Johnson.

NOTES ON *THE DESERTED VILLAGE*

The Deserted Village was published May 26, 1770. Like
The Traveler, it had been long in the thoughts of its author,
and had been rewritten, revised, and polished with the care
which his poems always received. Unlike *The Traveler*, it
won immediate popularity, five editions being called for
within three months. It excited Goethe's youthful enthusi-
asm, and won from the poet Gray, grown old and hypercritical,
the exclamation, "This man is a poet!" An account of its com-
position will be found on page twenty-two of the Introduction.

The meter of *The Deserted Village* is the heroic couplet of
which Goldsmith had made such masterly use in *The Traveler;*
in *The Deserted Village* it received new ease, grace, and charm.

The didactic theme of the poem had already been touched
upon in *The Traveler;* it is the evils of luxury and the miseries
of the poor in a rich commercial country. Goldsmith con-
founds commerce and wealth with luxury, condemning all
three as evils; he states as a fact — what statistics disprove—
that England was becoming depopulated; and he sees only
misery ahead of the emigrants leaving the Old World for the
New. The truth or falsehood of these statements does not
affect our pleasure in the poems and its beautiful descriptions
of the little village in its prosperity and its decay. In "Sweet
Auburn," Goldsmith described, softened and beautified by
the light of memory, his childhood's home, the Irish village
of Lissoy. Macaulay, an English author, remarks: "The
village in its happy days is a true English village. The village
in its decay is an Irish village. The felicity and the misery
which Goldsmith has brought close together belong to two
different countries and to two different stages in the progress
of society. He had assuredly never seen in his native island
such a rural paradise, such a seat of plenty, content, and
tranquillity, as his Auburn. He had assuredly never seen in
England all the inhabitants of such a paradise turned out of
their homes in one day and forced to emigrate in a body to

America. The hamlet he had probably seen in Kent; the ejectment he had probably seen in Munster; but by joining the two he has produced something which never was and never will be seen in any part of the world."

The poet, however, was not endeavoring to give a guide-book description of any one village, English or Irish. He sought poetic truth and dramatic contrast and attained them with unerring instinct; in our hearts, "sweet Auburn" has a reality vouchsafed to few villages duly indicated on the map.

The Traveler was dedicated to Goldsmith's brother Henry and *The Deserted Village* to his friend, Sir Joshua Reynolds. These dedications are proofs — if proofs be needed — of the manly independence of the poet. It was usual in that day for authors to dedicate their works to some noble or powerful patron, whose favor they wished to court; but Goldsmith inscribed his poems, as tokens of affection, to his brother and his friend.

1. **Auburn:** Goldsmith's native village, Lissoy in Ireland, is supposed to be the original of the village of Auburn. The name Auburn was suggested by his friend, Bennet Langton.

2. **Swain:** See note on *The Traveler*, line 48.

3. **Smiling spring:** What figure of speech is here used?

4. **Parting:** Departing; compare the first line of Gray's *Elegy*:

"The curfew tolls the knell of parting day."

5-15. "Ten lines, from the fifth to the fifteenth, had been his second morning's work; and when Cooke entered his chamber he read them to him aloud. 'Come,' he added, 'let me tell you this is no bad morning's work; and now, my dear boy, if you are not better engaged, I should be glad to enjoy Shoemaker's Holiday with you.'" — *Forster*.

6. **Seats:** Abodes, — as in the expression, 'country seat.'

9. Express the meaning of this line in your own words.

10. **Cot:** Cottage.

12. **Decent:** Adapted to the purpose for which it was made; becoming. This is the meaning of the Latin word from which 'decent' is derived, and is the sense in which it was commonly used during the eighteenth century.

15. **The coming day:** Some holiday, when the village green was the scene of rustic merry-making.

17. **Train:** Long-drawn-out line of villagers. Notice how frequently Goldsmith uses the word in this poem.

19. **Circled:** The word here has the force of 'went round,' three lines below.

20. **Contending:** Striving for superiority in the games going on.

22. **Sleight:** Cunning trick. We use the word now chiefly in the expression, 'sleight of hand.'

Feat: Act showing skill, strength, or courage. The word means literally 'something done.'

23. **Tired:** That is, tired those who joined in it.

25. **Simply:** In a simple manner.

27. **Mistrustless:** Unconscious of. Explain the meaning of this and the following line.

34. **Lawn:** Plain; the word formerly denoted an open space in a woodland, but now generally denotes the grassy space in front of a house.

37. **Tyrant:** Here used to describe a wealthy land-owner who turned people off his estate. It is thought that Goldsmith referred to General Robert Napier, who expelled several families from his estate near Lissoy.

39. **Only:** Observe the force of this adjective.

40. Only half the land is tilled or cultivated, and thus the plain is deprived of its former beauty and luxuriance.

43. **Glades:** Open spaces in woods; literally, places through which light glitters.

44. **Bittern:** A wading bird of the heron species. Goldsmith says in his *Animated Nature*, "Of all these sounds there is none so dismally hollow as the booming of the bittern."

45. **Lapwing:** Plover or pewit.

50. Is the scene described in lines 35–50 more or less impressive because it follows the description of the village in its days of happiness and prosperity? Give reasons for your opinion.

51. **Fares the land:** Goes it with the land.

52. **Decay:** Decrease in numbers or pass away.

51–52. Goldsmith expresses the same thought in the nineteenth chapter of *The Vicar of Wakefield*.

54. **A breath:** That is, a mere word.
The Scotch poet, Robert Burns, later expressed this same thought in the words:

"Princes and lords are but the breath of kings."

55. **Peasantry:** Country population as opposed to town.

57. Goldsmith represents Auburn as an English village; he describes conditions which he thought were common to England and Ireland.

58. **Rood:** Is this word used in its literal sense of one fourth of an acre? What is its meaning here?

63. Goldsmith makes the mistake of confusing trade with luxury, and wealth with oppression. We love and admire this poem, but we realize that some of its opinions and theories are wrong.

64. **Usurp:** The verb agrees with the plural idea instead of the singular form of its subject, 'train.'

69. What is the subject of 'bade'?

74. **Manners:** Customs.

79. **Many a year elapsed:** After the lapse of many years.

Return: Goldsmith never did return to the Irish home which he left in 1752. His letters express this same pathetic desire to go back to his childhood's home, to sit again by "Lissoy fireside," and "be placed on the Little Mount before Lissoy gate, and there take in, to me, the most pleasing horizon in nature."

81. **Train:** That is, of thoughts and memories.

87. **Husband out:** Use with economy.

87–88. Express this thought in your own words.

89–96. "A city like this is the soil for great virtues and great vices. . . . There are no pleasures, sensual or sentimental, which this city does not produce; yet I know not how I could be content to reside here for life. There is something so seducing in that spot in which we first had existence, that nothing but it can please. Whatever vicissitudes we experience in life, however we toil, or wherever we wander, our fatigued wishes still recur to home for tranquillity; we long to die in that spot which gave us birth, and in that pleasing expectation find an opiate for every calamity." — Goldsmith in *The Citizen of the World*.

93. **An:** See note on *The Traveler*, line 34.

Whom: Can you give any reason for the poet's use of 'whom' instead of 'which'?

98. To what does 'that' refer?

101–102. Goldsmith expressed a similar thought in a prose essay: " By struggling with misfortune we are sure to receive some wound in the conflict: the only method to come off victorious is by running away."

106. **Imploring famine:** One suffering from famine who implores aid; a beggar.

107. **Latter end:** See Job viii, 7.

110. Sir Joshua Reynolds painted a picture of Resignation and had an engraving made from it upon which were inscribed some lines from *The Deserted Village*, and these words: "This attempt to express a character in *The Deserted Village* is dedicated to Dr. Goldsmith by his sincere friend and admirer, Joshua Reynolds."

113. **Evening:** Afternoon, the sense in which it is commonly used in the southern states.

117. **Responsive:** Answering back by singing.

118. **To meet:** That is, at meeting, — like the Latin gerund.

122. **Spoke:** Bespoke; indicated.

Vacant: Empty or free of thought or care, not necessarily of intelligence.

124. **Nightingale:** This bird is not found in Ireland.

126. **Fluctuate:** Rise and fall.

Gale: Here, a breeze; a gentle, not a strong wind.

129. This is a character from real life. The cabin of Catherine Geraghty was long pointed out near Lissoy, and the brook close by, mantled with cresses.

130. **Plashy:** Puddle-like.

131. **Bread:** In what sense is this word here used?

132. **Cresses:** Water-cress. Why are 'cresses' called 'mantling'?

133. **Wintry:** For use during the winter.

137–192. These lines were written soon after the poet received the news of the death of his brother Henry, at Athlone, Ireland, in May, 1768.

139. **Disclose:** Show, mark.

140–192. **Village preacher:** In this description Goldsmith is thought to have had in mind his father and his brother Henry, and possible also his uncle Contarine, all of whom were clergymen in Irish villages. Commit to memory part or all of this description.

Mansion: We restrict this word to a dwelling of large size, but in Goldsmith's time it was applied to any house, meaning only a place of abode.

141. **Country:** Neighborhood.

142. **Passing:** Surpassingly; exceedingly.

Forty pounds: About the middle of the eighteenth century, forty pounds, about two hundred dollars, was the sum of many a country parson's income; the purchasing value of money was then greater than now.

144. **Place:** Position in life.

155. **Broken:** Broken down, by hardships or age.

157. What is the meaning of 'done' here?

159. Express this thought in your own words.

162. He gave from pity, or sympathy, before he considered the duty, or charity, of doing so.

173. **Champion:** Literally, one who fights in single com-

bat; here, the clergyman is represented as contending against
sin, or the power of evil.

176. **Accents:** Words, — a common poetical use of the
word.

179. **Double sway:** Double power, because he taught by
both precept and example.

184. **His gown:** Clergymen then habitually went to
church in the black gowns which they wore while preaching.

189–192. A sublime simile, describing the village preacher's
position in his little world.

193–218. The village schoolmaster is thought to be a
picture of Goldsmith's teacher, Thomas, or 'Paddy,' Byrne.
This is another passage that you should commit to memory.

194. **Furze:** A thorny evergreen shrub, that bears bright
yellow blossoms. Why does Goldsmith call it "unprofitably
gay"?

199. **Boding:** Foreboding; foreseeing evil.

207. **Village:** What does the word mean here?

209. **Terms:** Periods in which law-courts and colleges are
in session; also, the times when rents are settled.

Tides: This usually means the times of high and low
water; here, it probably means times or seasons, the old
meaning of the word which still survives in the words
Whitsuntide, Eastertide, noontide, etc.

Presage: Foretell.

210. **Gauge:** Measure the capacities of vessels, such as
barrels and hogsheads.

221. **Nut-brown draughts:** Drinks of brown ale; the "nut
brown ale" of the poets.

222. **Graybeard mirth and smiling toil:** Mirthful old men
and smiling workmen.

227. **Nicely-sanded:** It was then a common custom to
sprinkle floors with sand, often marked in patterns.

232. **Twelve good rules:** These rules, ascribed to Charles I.,
were hung up in most inns in Goldsmith's time. They were:
"1. Urge no healths. 2. Profane no divine ordinances.

3. Touch no state matters. 4. Reveal no secrets. 5. Pick no quarrels. 6. Make no companions. 7. Maintain no ill opinions. 8. Keep no bad company. 9. Encourage no vice. 10. Make no long meals. 11. Repeat no grievances. 12. Lay no wagers."

232. **Game of goose:** A game somewhat like checkers, played on a board on certain squares of which a goose was depicted.

234. **Gay:** This adjective describes 'hearth.'

236. **Chimney:** Fireplace.

243. **Farmer's news:** News gathered on his visits to markets.

Barber's tale: Barbers are proverbially talkative.

244. **Woodman's ballad:** Narrative poem or popular song, probably about Robin Hood. In Goldsmith's time 'woodman' meant usually 'huntsman.'

248. **Mantling bliss:** Foaming ale.

250. **Kiss the cup:** Touch it with her lips.

259. **Pomp:** Here used in its original sense of train, procession.

265–285. In these lines Goldsmith expresses his opinion that trade is a disadvantage to the poor. He says that the wealthy enlarge their estates by gaining possession of the small farms, on which lived the poorer classes. These country people, deprived of homes and means of support, were forced to emigrate. \ Do you agree with Goldsmith in thinking that trade, bringing prosperity and wealth, is a disadvantage to a country? Give reasons for your opinion.

267–268. Goldsmith says in *The Citizen of the World:* "There is a wide difference between a conquering and a flourishing empire."

276. **That many poor supplied:** That supplied many poor people with homes and means of support.

284. **For:** That is, to be exchanged for. Goldsmith assumes that products needed at home are exported to procure luxuries that are superfluous.

287. **Female:** This use of the word where we would say 'woman ' was common in Goldsmith's day.

Plain: That is, in dress.

288. **Secure to please:** Confident of pleasing.

293. **Solicitous to bless:** Anxious to charm.

294. Express this thought in your own words.

295. See note on line 51.

300. **Band:** Family.

302. **A garden and a grave:** A pleasure-garden for the rich, but for the poor a 'grave,' in which is buried their former happiness.

304. **Scape:** Escape, — not a contraction, but a word used in prose and verse.

305–308. The enclosure of the Commons, or public lands, was regarded as a grievance by the poor, though it was often useful and sometimes necessary.

308. **Bare-worn:** Worn bare of grass.

316. **Artist:** Artisan; workman. In Goldsmith's time, 'artist' was often used to designate one who practiced the useful or mechanic arts, while 'artisan' was used to denote one who practiced the fine arts, such as painting and sculpture.

318. **Gibbet:** In the eighteenth century, the gallows was erected on the highway and evil-doers were executed publicly, to serve as a warning. Do you think this was a wise custom?

319. **Dome:** See note on *The Traveler*, line 159.

322. **Torches:** Before street lights were introduced into London, well-to-do people going abroad at night were accompanied by men or boys bearing torches. These were usually made of twisted tow, dipped in pitch.

323. **Sure:** Surely.

329. **Might adorn:** That is, might have adorned.

335. **Idly:** Here used in its old sense of foolishly.

Ambitious of the town: Longing for a city life.

336. **Wheel:** Spinning-wheel. In Goldsmith's time, spinning was one of the regular household duties of women.

341–358. Goldsmith's fancy painted a gloomy picture of

the regions in the New World, to which the peasants emigrated. Most Englishmen of the eighteenth century had vague or incorrect ideas about America. Goldsmith describes the tropical regions depicted by early travelers, as if they were the ones in which Englishmen usually settled. Is this in accordance with facts?

344. Altama: The Altamaha River, in Georgia. You have read in the history of the United States about the colony which General Oglethorpe established in Georgia for poor debtors. General Oglethorpe was one of Goldsmith's friends, and no doubt spoke to him of the colony, but probably not in the gloomy terms used here by the poet.

349. Matted: All the earlier travelers in America spoke of the impenetrable growth of tangled underwood which they found in the forests.

350. Silent bats: In tropical regions, bats cluster together and suspend themselves by their hind legs to the branches of trees. Thus they remain during the day, asleep in masses.

352. Gathers death: Collects deadly venom.

354. The rattle-snake is the most dreaded of all American snakes.

355. The tiger, and even the jaguar which is sometimes called 'the American tiger,' are unknown on the banks of the Altamaha.

356. Savage men: Indians.

360. Grassy-vested: Clothed with grass.

361. Warbling grove: The grove in which birds are warbling.

362. Thefts: Such as the stealing of a kiss.

363-384. Goldsmith sees only the grief of the peasants at leaving their native land. It does not occur to him that they may make homes and find happiness in another land.

368. Western Main: What ocean is meant?

Seats: See note on line 6.

379. Plaints: Complaints.

386. Things like these: What things are meant?

387. **Potions:** Drafts; drinks.

393. **Sapped:** Undermined.

399. **Anchoring:** Lying at anchor.

402. Goldsmith makes a distinction, not usual nor, indeed, necessary, between 'shore' and 'strand'; he limits 'strand' to the strip of beach lying between the ocean and the main 'shore.'

411. **Nymph:** Here applied to poetry. In Greek mythology, nymphs were inferior divinities.

412. **Solitary:** That is, when alone.

415. **Noble arts:** The fine arts, such as music, painting, and sculpture.

418. **Torno's cliffs:** Probably the cliffs around Lake Tornea, in the northern part of Sweden.

Pambamarca: A height of the Andes Mountains, near Quito.

422. Make up for the rigors of an inclement climate.

424. **Of:** For.

428. **Mole:** A mound or breakwater at the mouth of a harbor.

427–430. Boswell tells us that the last four lines of this poem were added by Dr. Samuel Johnson, who thought that it ended too tamely as completed by Goldsmith.

NOTES ON *THE HERMIT*

The old English ballad poetry was neglected while the formal verse of Dryden and Pope was in favor. It had, however, always some friends and admirers, one of whom was Goldsmith's friend, Bishop Percy. He collected the old ballads and published them under the title of *Reliques of Ancient English Poetry*, and he was so saturated with that kind of literature that he wrote several poems in the style of the old ballads. Goldsmith, too, liked the old poems, and about 1764 he tried his hand at a ballad, which he liked better than any other poem he wrote. "As to my 'Hermit,'" he said, "that poem cannot be amended." It was shown to the Countess of Northumberland, for whom it was probably written, and was privately printed for her in the year 1765. It was entitled: *Edwin and Angelina, a Ballad by Mr. Goldsmith: Printed for the Amusement of the Countess of Northumberland.* This poem was first brought before the public in 1766, under the title of *The Hermit*, in the thirteenth chapter of *The Vicar of Wakefield.* Goldsmith was accused of having taken the poem from Bishop Percy's *Friar of Orders Gray*, published in 1765. In a letter in *St. James Chronicle*, Goldsmith disproved this charge. He said: "Another correspondent of yours accuses me of having taken a ballad I published some time ago from one by the ingenious Mr. Percy. I do not think there is any great resemblance between the two pieces in question. If there be any, his ballad is taken from mine. I read it to Mr. Percy some years ago; and he (as we both considered these things as trifles at best) told me with his usual good humor, the next time I saw him, that he had taken my plan to form the fragments of Shakespeare into a ballad of his own. He then read me his little Cento, if I may so call it, and I highly approved it. Such petty anecdotes as these are scarce worth printing: and, were it not for the busy disposition of some of your correspondents, the public should never have known that he owes me the hint of his ballad, or that I am obliged to his friendship and learning for communications of a much more important nature."

11. **Faithless phantom:** A willow-o'-the-wisp.

19. **Rushy:** Of rushes.

27. **Scrip:** An old word, meaning a small bag.

31–32. The line referred to here is found in Young's *Night Thoughts:*

"Man wants but little nor that little long."

In *The Citizen of the World*, Goldsmith quotes the line correctly. Does the meter of *The Hermit* suggest to you any reason why Goldsmith may have altered the line intentionally?

51. **Legendary lore:** Knowledge of old times.
57–60. In the first edition this stanza read:

> "But nothing mirthful could assuage
> The pensive stranger's woe;
> For grief had seized his early age,
> And tears would often flow."

How did the poet's changes improve the lines?
80. **Turtle:** Turtle-dove.
84. In the first edition, this line was:

> "The bashful guest betrayed."

87. This line originally was:

> "Like clouds that deck the morning skies."

Why is 'colors' a better word here than 'clouds'?
97–104. In the first edition these lines were:

> "Forgive, and let thy pious care
> A heart's distress allay;
> That seeks repose, but finds despair
> Companion of the way.

> "My father liv'd, of high degree,
> Remote beside the Tyne;
> And as he had but only me,
> Whate'er he had was mine.

> "To win me from his tender arms,
> Unnumber'd suitors came;
> Their chief pretence my flatter'd charms,
> My wealth perhaps their aim."

101. **Tyne:** The river Tyne flows through Northumberland. The poem had thus for the Countess of Northumberland an additional interest from having its scene laid there.
117–120. This stanza was not written till some years after

the remainder of the poem, and was presented, in manuscript, to a Richard Archdal, Esq. It was first printed in the poem in Bishop Percy's edition in 1801.

125–128. "The gentle but exquisite beauty of these stanzas is truly Goldsmithian."

133 *et seq.* In the first edition these lines were:

"Till quite dejected with my scorn,
    He left me to deplore;
And sought a solitude forlorn,
    And ne'er was heard of more.

"Then since he perish'd by my fault
    This pilgrimage I pay;
I'll seek the solitude he sought,
    And stretch me where he lay.

"And there in shelt'ring thickets hid,
    I'll linger till I die;
'Twas thus for me my lover did,
    And so for him will I."

"Thou shalt not thus," the Hermit cried,
    And clasp'd her to his breast;
The astonish'd fair one turned to chide, —
    'Twas Edwin's self that prest,

For now no longer could he hide,
    What first to hide he strove;
His looks resume their youthful pride,
    And flush with honest love.

160. In the first edition, there followed two stanzas which Goldsmith omitted because they were not needed by the action of the poem. These stanzas are:

"Here amidst sylvan bowers we'll rove,
    From lawn to woodland stray;
Blest as the songsters of the grove,
    And innocent as they.

"To all that want, and all that wail,
  Our pity shall be given;
And when this life of love shall fail,
  We'll love again in heaven."

NOTES ON *DESCRIPTION OF AN AUTHOR'S BEDCHAMBER*

These lines are slightly altered from a poetical passage sent in a letter to his brother Henry in 1759. Compare them with lines 227–236 of *The Deserted Village*. Most of the difficult expressions have already been explained in the notes on that passage.

14. William, Duke of Cumberland, was the hero of the Battle of Culloden, fought in 1746. He defeated the Highland troops, destroying the Stuarts' last hope of regaining the English crown.

NOTES ON *AN ELEGY ON THE DEATH OF A MAD DOG*

This ballad was first printed in 1766, in the seventeenth chapter of *The Vicar of Wakefield*, but it was probably written some years before. In *The Citizen of the World*, Goldsmith "ridicules the fear of mad dogs as one of the epidemic terrors to which the people of England are occasionally prone."

5. **Islington:** A district of London, where Goldsmith lived from 1762 to 1764. It was then, as he described it in *The Citizen of the World*, "a pretty, neat town, mostly built of brick, with a church and bells; it has a small lake, or rather pond, in the midst."

NOTES ON *AN ELEGY ON THAT GLORY OF HER SEX, MRS. MARY BLAIZE*

These amusing verses were first printed in 1759, in *The Bee*, a periodical by Goldsmith. The idea of this, as of several other of Goldsmith's minor poems, is taken from the French, but the poet improves upon the original.

26. **Kent Street:** When Goldsmith first went to London in 1756, he practiced medicine at Southwark; "Kent Street, then sacred to beggars and broom men, traverses Southwark."

NOTES ON *WHEN LOVELY WOMAN STOOPS TO FOLLY*

This song was first printed in 1766, in the twenty-fourth chapter of *The Vicar of Wakefield*. It is sung by Olivia Primrose, who has been deserted by her lover. "The charm of the words and the graceful way in which they are introduced seem to have blinded criticism to the impropriety and even inhumanity of requiring poor Olivia to sing a song so completely applicable to her own case," says Dobson. To most people, however, the incident seems pleasing and not inappropriate in Goldsmith's graceful world of fancy.

NOTES ON *THE WRETCH CONDEMNED WITH LIFE TO PART*, AND *O MEMORY, THOU FOND DECEIVER*

These two songs were first published in 1776, two years after Goldsmith's death. They are songs in *The Captivity: An Oratorio*. It was written in 1764, and set to music, but not performed; it was not published until 1820. Of *The Wretch Condemned with Life to Part*, Irving says: "Most of *The Oratorio* has passed into oblivion; but the following song from it will never die."

NOTES ON *STANZAS ON THE TAKING OF QUEBEC*

This poem was first printed in 1759, in *The Busy Body*. It is written, not in the heroic couplets which Goldsmith generally used, but in 'heroic quatrains,' the stanza which Gray used in his *Elegy Written in a Country Churchyard.*

Give an account of the historical event which suggested this poem to the patriotic Goldsmith.

NOTES ON *THE HAUNCH OF VENISON*

Part of the spring and summer of 1771, Goldsmith passed in Essex and at Bath with his friend and countryman, Lord Clare. Soon after this visit, Lord Clare sent the poet a gift of venison and received in return these charming humorous verses. Forster says: "If Lord Clare had sent an entire buck every season to his friend's humble chambers in the Temple, the single 'Haunch of Venison' which Goldsmith sent back would richly have repaid him. The charming verses which bear that name were written this year (1771), and appear to have been written for Lord Clare alone; nor was it until two years after their writer's death that they obtained a wider audience than his immediate circle of friends. Yet written with no higher aim than of private pleasantry, a more delightful piece of humor, or a more finished bit of style, has probably been seldom written. There is not a word to spare, every word is in its right place, the most boisterous animal spirits are controlled by the most charming good taste, and an indescribable airy elegance pervades and encircles all. Its very incidents seem of right to claim a place here, so naturally do they fall within the drama of Goldsmith's life."

We are informed that 'the leading idea of *The Haunch of Venison* is taken from a poem by Boileau, a French poet, and some passages which seem most original are copied from the French satire.'

8. **Virtu:** An object of art.

9–12. This is said to be a custom in Ireland, — and in other countries, according to Goldsmith. In *Animated Nature,* he says: — "There is scarcely a cottage in Germany, Poland, and Switzerland, that is not hung round with these marks of hospitality; and which often makes the owner better contented with hunger, since he has it in his power to be luxurious, when he thinks proper. A piece of beef hung up there, is considered as an elegant piece of furniture, which, though seldom touched, at least argues the possessor's opulence and ease."

18. **Mr. Byrne:** A nephew of Lord Clare's.

21. **Reynolds:** His friend, Sir Joshua Reynolds.

24. **M—r—s:** Monroe's; Miss Dorothy Monroe was a belle of the day.

27. Howard's identity is unknown; Coley was probably Colman, a dramatist; Hogarth is said to have been a London surgeon; Hiff was a Dr. Paul Hiffernan, an author, poor in every sense of the word, who often made demands on Goldsmith's purse.

29. **Higgins:** An Irish friend of Goldsmith's.

34. In a letter which Goldsmith wrote to his brother, Maurice, in 1770, we find the same expression: "Honors to one in my situation are something like ruffles to one that wants a shirt." This was just after the king had made him professor of Ancient History in the Royal Academy, a position to which no salary was attached.

37–38. In the first published copy, these lines read:

"A fine-spoken custom-house officer he,
 Who smiled as he gazed on the Venison and me."

It is suggested that these lines described a real person and were changed to conceal his identity.

49. **Johnson:** Dr. Samuel Johnson, mentioned so often before in this volume.

Burke: The distinguished statesman, Goldsmith's countryman and friend.

55. **Mile-end:** A district of London.

60. This is said to be a quotation from a letter Henry, Duke of Cumberland, wrote to Lady Grosvenor.

72. **Thrale:** A wealthy London brewer; he and his wife were intimate friends of Dr. Johnson's.

78. 'Cinna,' 'Panurge': Dr. Scott, a political writer of Goldsmith's day, wrote under these pen-names. Cinna was a Roman consul, and Panurge is the rogue in a romance by the French author, Rabelais.

108–109. Priam the king of Troy. These lines were suggested by a passage in Shakespeare's *Henry IV.*, Part II.:

"Even such a man, so faint, so spiritless,
So dull, so dead in look, so wo-begone,
Drew Priam's curtains in the dead of night,
And would have told him half his Troy was burned;
But Priam found the fire ere he his tongue."

114. Philomel: According to Greek legend, Philomela was changed to a nightingale.

117. One of your taste: Lord Clare was himself a wit and a poet.

NOTES ON *RETALIATION*

This poem was written in February, 1774, only a few weeks before Goldsmith's death. It was left unfinished, and was not published until after the poet's death. On page twenty-four of the Introduction is given an account of the incident which suggested it.

1. Scarron: A French comic writer of the seventeenth century, to whose dinners people brought dishes, as to a picnic.

3. Landlord: The master of the St. James Coffee-house, where Goldsmith and his friends here mentioned sometimes dined.

5. Dean: Dr. Barnard, Dean of Derry, a well-known wit of the day, who wrote some very good verses in response to this poem.

6. Burke: The famous orator and stateman, Edmund Burke.

7. Will: William Burke, a kinsman of the orator's.

8. Dick: Richard Burke, a younger brother of Edmund's.

9. **Cumberland:** Richard Cumberland, an author of the day, who wrote poems, novels, and dramas.

10. **Douglas:** Dr. John Douglas, a scholarly Scotchman who was afterwards Bishop of Salisbury.

11. **Garrick:** David Garrick, the famous actor, whose mock epitaph on Goldsmith provoked this poem.

14. **Ridge:** Counselor John Ridge, an Irish lawyer.

Reynolds: Sir Joshua Reynolds, who was probably Goldsmith's dearest friend.

15. **Hickey:** Thomas Hickey, an Irish lawyer, well known for his hospitality and good humor.

16. Notice Goldsmith's humorous characterization of himself.

29–42. "We then spoke of *Retaliation*," says Northcote, "and praised the character of Burke in particular as a masterpiece. Nothing that he had ever said or done but what was foretold in it: nor was he painted as the principal figure in the foreground with the partiality of a friend, or as the great man of the day, but with a background of history, showing both what he was and what he might have been."

Tommy Townshend: Thomas Townshend, a member of Parliament; he afterward became Lord Sydney.

38. **Nice:** Scrupulous.

41. **Mutton cold:** Burke often came late to meals, owing to the length of his speeches which detained him in Parliament.

43. **William:** See note on line 7.

51. **Richard:** See note on line 8.

54. Richard Burke had recently broken his leg.

62. **Terence:** A Roman comic poet of the second century before Christ. His plays lack originality, but are remarkable for beauty of style.

67. **Dizened:** Bedizened is the more common form of this word, which means dressed up, bedecked.

68. **Rout:** A fashionable name, in the eighteenth century, for an evening gathering.

86. **Dodds:** Rev. Dr. William Dodd was a fashionable preacher who was hanged for forgery in 1777.

Kenrick: Dr. Kenrick was known in his day as a lecturer and dramatist, but is now only remembered for his scurrilous abuse of Goldsmith.

87. **Macpherson:** A Scotch author who wrote the *Poems of Ossian,* and persuaded many people that they were old Keltic poems. Goldsmith here refers to his prose translation of Homer.

89. **Landers:** William Landers was a Scotchman, author of a literary forgery, charging Milton with plagiarism; this was exposed by Dr. Douglas.

Bowers: Archibald Bowers, a Scotchman, who wrote a *History of the Popes,* containing errors and plagiarisms which were pointed out by Dr. Douglas.

93–124. "The portrait of David Garrick is one of the most elaborate in the poem. When the poet came to touch it off, he had some lurking piques to gratify, which the recent attack had revived. He may have forgotten David's cavalier treatment of him in the early days of his comparative obscurity; he may have forgiven his refusal of his plays; but Garrick had been capricious in his conduct in the times of their recent intercourse: sometimes treating him with gross familiarity, at other times affecting dignity and reserve, and assuming airs of superiority; frequently he had been facetious and witty in company at his expense, and lastly he had been guilty of the couplet just quoted. Goldsmith, therefore, touched off the lights and shadows of his character with a free hand, and, at the same time, gave a side hit at his old rival, Kelly, and his critical persecutor, Kenrick, in making them sycophantic satellites of the actor. Goldsmith, however, was void of gall even in his revenge, and his very satire was more humorous than caustic." — *Washington Irving.*

115. **Kelly:** Hugh Kelly, an Irish writer of essays, poems, and plays, was Goldsmith's chief rival as a dramatist. His *False Delicacy* was acted about the same time that Gold-

smith's *Good-natured Man* was played, and Kelly's comedy had by far the greater success. It is now almost forgotten.

Woodfall: William Woodfall, the editor of *The Morning Chronicle*, and a well-known dramatic critic.

116. **Commerce:** Exchange of flattery.

117. **Grub-Street:** Now Milton Street, London. During the sixteenth and seventeenth centuries, Grub Street was the popular abiding place of literary men, but in the eighteenth century it was given over to the inferior class of authors.

118. **Be-Rosciused:** Praised as being a second Roscius; Roscius was the greatest of the Roman actors.

124. **Beaumonts:** Francis Beaumont was a famous dramatist of the Elizabethan age.

Bens: Ben Johnson was a dramatist of the Elizabethan age, second only to Shakespeare.

131. **Flat:** Without an opinion of his own.

140. **Bland:** "A word eminently happy and characteristic of his easy and placid manner." — *Malone.*

145. **Raphaels:** Raphael, the most popular of all the great Italian painters of the fifteenth and sixteenth centuries.

Correggios: Correggio was another Italian painter, who flourished at the time of Raphael.

146. **Trumpet:** Reynolds was so deaf that he had to use an ear-trumpet.

147. We are told that these were the last lines that Goldsmith wrote, and death found him with them unfinished. It was fitting that his last words should be a portrait of his friend, Sir Joshua. It is said that when the news of Goldsmith's death was brought him, Reynolds laid down his brush and painted no more that day, — a thing that he had never before done, even in times of affliction.

Postscript: This was first printed in the fifth edition of the poem. Goldsmith had given the lines to a friend, who sent a copy to the publisher in 1774.

148. **Whitefoord:** Mr. Caleb Whitefoord, a Scotchman who came to London and was for many years a wine merchant.

He was a notorious punster, and wrote much in prose and verse.

149. For this pun, see *Romeo and Juliet*, 3, 1.

155. **Bon mots:** Witticisms

161. See *Hamlet*, 5, 1.

163. See note on line 115.

171. These are the names of some of Whitefoord's humorous writings

EXAMINATION QUESTIONS

ON

THE DESERTED VILLAGE

BY

Cornelia Beare, Instructor in English, High School, White Plains, N. Y.

PRELIMINARY.

Consult Irving's Life of Goldsmith for account of early home and parents.

From "Vicar of Wakefield." Study character of the Vicar; description of the Primrose family's home in the country; injustice done to the poor by the rich, as shown by story of Squire Thornhill and Olivia. Story of Goldsmith's life, as given in Painter's English Literature.

PLAN OF STUDY FOR ABSOLUTE POSSESSION.

1. Divide the poem into sections, read in class and then write out the paraphrase of each as a chapter with its title indicating its theme.

(1) ll. 1–34	(7) ll. 237–264
(2) ll. 35–74	(8) ll. 265–302
(3) ll. 75–112	(9) ll. 303–336
(4) ll. 113–136	(10) ll. 337–384
(5) ll. 137–192	(11) ll. 385–430
(6) ll. 193–236	

2. Commit to memory.

(1) ll. 51–62	(5) ll. 193–216
(2) ll. 83–112	(6) ll. 265–286
(3) ll. 163–170	(7) ll. 415–430
(4) ll. 177–192	

EXERCISES IN DESCRIPTION.

1. A circumstantial description of Auburn as Goldsmith knew it in his boyhood.

2. A dynamic description emphasizing the simple happiness of the village.

3. An impressionistic description of the parson, from the view point of the villagers. Write as one of them.

4. Describe the inn as the schoolmaster would; try to talk as you think he would. (Use dictionary and book of synonyms for help.)

5. Describe the mansion and estate which has replaced Auburn. Use a moving point of view, and underscore transitions by which you make your change evident.

EXERCISES IN NARRATION.

1. In the person of a village lad, tell of a holiday eve at Auburn.

2. Let the same lad give an account of the doings in school.

3. Let the parson tell of a visit to a sick man of the village.

4. Let "the sad historian of the pensive plain," tell of the departure of the villagers.

5. Let one of the exiles tell of her struggles in the city and of her life in the new world.

EXERCISES IN EXPOSITION.

1. Explain the meaning of

(a) "Every pang that folly pays to pride."

(b) "Unpractised he to fawn or seek for power
By declines fashioned to the varying hour."

(c) "The country blooms — a garden and a grave."

(d) "Thou guide by which the nobler arts excel,
Thou nurse of every virtue."

2. Explain why Auburn was at first so happy.

3. Explain by analogy how a nation may be splendid, yet ready to fall to pieces.

4. Explain Goldsmith's personal grief in the ruin of Auburn.

ARGUMENT.

1. Prove that riches are not always a curse to a land.

2. Prepare a brief for your argument.

3. Collect Goldsmith's arguments to prove that the rich are responsible for the destruction of the country.

4. Arrange these in a brief.

5. Write argument from given brief.